RETIRING WITH ATTITUDE

Approaching and Relishing your Retirement

Caroline Lodge
and Eileen Carnell

guardianbooks

Published by Guardian Books 2014

2 4 6 8 10 9 7 5 3 1

First published in Great Britain in 2014 by
Guardian Books
Kings Place, 90 York Way
London N1 9GU

www.guardianbooks.co.uk

A CIP catalogue record for this book is available from the British Library

ISBN 978-0852-65558-0

Cover design by Two Associates
Typeset by seagulls.net

Printed in England by CPI Group (UK) Ltd, Croydon CR0 4YY

MIX
Paper from
responsible sources
FSC® C020471
FSC
www.fsc.org

Contents

A Note on Sources and Acknowledgements

Throughout the book we have drawn on many people's stories. We would like to thank all of those people who took part in our research and provided material for our book; in particular: the members of our retiring group Marianne Coleman, Jennifer Evans, Anne Gold, Allie Kirton, Anne Peters and Diane Leonard who provided an important forum for discussion and support over the last six years; the people who attended our retiring courses and coaching sessions; the retirees and former colleagues who were interviewed or who answered our questionnaires. They have made a rich contribution to the book and we are indebted to them. We have changed their names to guarantee confidentiality, unless their stories have already been published.

We are also grateful to the many readers of draft chapters, especially Marianne Coleman for reading all the chapters, and providing such helpful feedback and encouragement. Other readers included the many people who have attended our courses, and our friends, family and colleagues. Thanks are also due to Isobel Larkin for her inspiration, support and invaluable help as a source of research and connections.

Finally, we would like to thank all those at the *Guardian* who provided guidance and encouragement: the *Guardian* publisher Sara Montgomery, our editors Lindsay Davies and Katie Roden, the publishing executive Joanna Lord, Elena Fysentzou for copyediting, Jonathan Baker for the design, and all their other colleagues in the production team.

Introduction

This is the book we wanted to read when we started thinking about retiring. The available books we came across focused on pensions and told readers what to do. This book encourages you to consider your experiences much more widely than just your finances. It is written to help you manage the changes and transitions of retirement, and to help you forge the life you want well after you are no longer at work. Retirement, rather than being a waiting room for death, is a time of further exciting possibilities.

There is no single right way to approach any aspect of life, so our aim is not to be prescriptive; rather, we intend to encourage you to think ahead about your dreams and aspirations, shape the changes you experience and plan for 20 or more years of active, enjoyable and fulfilling life. We hope to convince you that:

- Previous images of retiring and retirement are redundant.
- Retirement is a series of transitions, rather than a single event. It's not the same from beginning to end.
- The majority of retirees are independent, active and contribute significantly to society.
- It's never too soon or too late to take action. It's good to plan ahead. Few decisions are irreversible.
- The beneficial aspects of work – including its structure, community, support and purpose – must be found in other activities in retirement.

- Ageism and sexism must be challenged.
- Learning is the most powerful means to handle changes and transitions.

These beliefs have been refined by our conversations with retirees attending workshops, coaching meetings, retiring groups and from research. And the following issues kept coming up when talking to them: changing images of retirement, gender inequalities and ageist attitudes, learning in retirement, transitions in retirement.

Changing Images and Understandings of Retirement

You probably take retirement for granted, but in some parts of the world it's actually unknown. In places like Okinawa (one of Japan's southern prefectures), the Hunza valley (a mountainous valley in Pakistan) and Vilcabamba (a city in Peru), people remain engaged and vigorous their whole lives. People age well in these communities. They remain active, and even into their nineties it is common for them to be walking several miles a day, gardening and caring for great-grandchildren. They have positive images of work and of becoming older, and there is no division in their lives between work and retirement. Long periods of chronic illness or disability are uncommon. They appear ageless.

Recent changes in our society mean that our culture and our views about retirement are changing. Past images of retirement are now redundant. There is a less acute division between work and retirement, and this may affect our experience. In some ways we may become more like the people of Okinawa and the Hunza valley.

Retirement was invented in the 19th century. It is a social construct just as 'old age' and 'childhood' are. The concept of retirement couldn't have existed had we not invented it, and we need not have invented retirement at all, at least not in its present form. Had we been a different kind of society, had we had different needs, values or interests, we might well have invented a different kind of entity, or constructed this one differently.

Today, retirement with a pension is considered a right for workers, and hard ideological, social and political battles are still being fought over it. In many western countries this right is guaranteed in national constitutions. Most developed countries provide pensions sponsored by employers and/or the state. In many less developed countries, as in the past, families provide support for older relatives.

And in the 21st century retirement is being re-invented, a response to the changing economic climate. Workers are expected to work for longer as they live to a greater age. In the UK, as well as in other places, the fixed retirement age has been axed so that people may choose to work for longer – a victory against ageism. At the same time, people may feel that they have been forced to work longer by alterations to pension payments, which has gone hand-in-hand with the removal of the fixed retirement age. Conceptions of what it is to be retired and the image of retirees have not yet caught up with the new version. The dominant conception of retirement remains linked with negative images of people who are no longer useful, get in the way, make no contribution to society, take up valuable housing space, become frail and have to stop work. Such inaccurate images must be challenged.

Gender Inequalities and Ageist Attitudes

The legacy from earlier times, especially beliefs and attitudes that allotted different roles to men and women, has resulted in different gender-based retirement experiences, despite more women now being active in the workforce. The main outcome is financial: women frequently have less substantial occupational and/or private pensions. This arises from their working history – they are more likely to have worked in part-time jobs, to have interrupted their careers to have children or to take care of family members, or to have worked in piecework and 'pink-collar' professions (such as teaching and nursing), which attract lower salaries and offer fewer opportunities for promotion.

In addition, women and men have different life expectancies. Women retiring at the age of 65 can expect to live at least another 19 years, three or four years longer than men retiring at the same age. The unavoidable conclusion is that women are likely to live more years in retirement, and they have longer to spend less. And because they live longer, women are more likely to spend their retirement years living on their own. But, women's experiences can be to their advantage. It is possible that they adjust better to life as a retired person, especially if they've had weaker attachments to their work.

A second unavoidable aspect of retirement is ageism. You may notice it in everyday language, which reinforces old-fashioned attitudes. Language related to retirees frequently refers to age, decrepitude and even some notion of deception: 'old-age pensioners', 'geriatrics', 'wrinklies', 'coffin dodgers'.

More toxic is the strand of ageism in political and social discourse. This blames our generation for the social and economic problems of the early 21st century, and especially for the economic difficulties experienced by the younger generation. It has been called 'the new ageism'.

An example of this new ageism is David Willetts' book *The Pinch: How the Baby Boomers Took Their Children's Future – And Why They Should Give it Back* – a clever title, implying both a financial squeeze and theft (he is a Conservative in the coalition government). The culprits can quickly be identified: people born between 1945 and 1965. The thesis of *The Pinch* is that this generation, sloppily labelled 'baby boomers', has broken an implicit contract between the generations. They have done too well from the welfare state, from property ownership, and are now 'absorbing more than their fair share of taxpayers' money', to use the ill-chosen words of the Bishop of London Richard Chartres.

There are some serious flaws with an argument that blames a whole generation. In the first place, the label 'baby boomer' does not comfortably apply to the working class, migrants, ethnic minorities, or those older people who currently live lonely lives in poverty. Many of the people being blamed are also, of course, taxpayers themselves, thus contributing to the very welfare state they're accused of draining. And further, it's a spurious analysis of the causes of complex social and economic problems to ascribe them to all the people born in a 20-year period.

In any case, the idea of the selfish generation hardly squares with the evidence that older people form the bedrock of what David Cameron calls the 'big society'. It is well documented that older people make a disproportionately large contribution to civic society, through volunteering, charitable giving, voting and other forms of civic engagement, from petitioning to becoming councillors. Older people volunteer, vote, donate and engage in the community more than other age groups.

Those who are fortunate within the older age group do help out the next generation in large numbers, thereby contradicting the image of selfish hoggers. Two-thirds of first-time buyers get help from their parents when buying their first home. More than 3 million young British adults aged 20–34 lived with their parents in 2013 (an increase of 25 per cent since 1996), according to official statistics. Many older people provide care for grandchildren, saving considerable sums on childcare fees for their sons and daughters, and they may care for older relatives too.

Understanding retirement's potential is very challenging in the context of such attitudes and legacies. Yet, there are many ways retirees can learn to shape their retirement, by constructing their understanding of events and changes and seeing themselves in new ways.

Learning in Retirement

Continuing to learn in your latter years is perhaps the key to building a successful retirement. Conflicting issues and disorienting dilemmas arise from life's changes. Learning from these experiences is the most powerful tool for handling transitions, as it means you are not helpless in the face of challenges and it can help you take control and create the life you want. You learn how to become a retired person. Your identity is actively constructed as you integrate new events into your own accounts of your life. Learning is challenging and getting support from others is invaluable. Collaborative learning can be especially fruitful.

This kind of learning involves reflecting on how you feel, becoming more aware of your communications and how you negotiate new situations. You can prepare to change, to discover new ways of seeing and behaving within the context of your family and community. You can develop resilience and robustness, and recognise patterns before they restrict your actions.

Most retirees strive to lead positive, productive and happy lives. Some of their success is down to luck, wealth or position. The bits that can be changed by individuals are likely to require the following activities:

- Connecting with people. Supporting and nurturing several close communities.
- Engaging in meaningful and purposeful activities. Getting involved in the things that matter to you.
- Finding intellectual and mental stimulation. Being open to learning and change.
- Self-reflection and insightfulness. Understanding ways of being and becoming.
- Maintaining good physical capabilities and well-being through activity. Keeping a healthy outlook.
- Being open to love and to being loved. Giving and receiving, and nurturing your closest relationships.
- Achieving a sense of fulfilment through creative endeavours.
- Laughing and singing.
- Openness to inspiration. Noticing and appreciating the beautiful, natural, built and created wonders of the world.

Retirees' Transitions

Transitions in retirement can be difficult for three reasons. First, they extend over several years, perhaps 20 or 30, beginning long before any retirement event and continuing well into older age. Second, they affect all aspects of life, including the social, physical and emotional. Third, retirees are currently making their adjustments in the difficult context of austerity, and in the face of gender inequalities and ageism.

Because work has a central role in life, the transition to a non-work-based identity is particularly challenging. Writing about his parents, the author Richard Ford captures the significance of a person's job in the eyes of both the worker and other people:

> A job meant who you were, it gave early indication of what you were worth, it suggested something about your character as a provider and what you valued, about your hold on a secure future, about your grasp on moral responsibility and self-awareness. It was an easy index (probably too easy) for what the world needed to know about you.

The significance of work means that you may find the transition from a work-based identity very hard to accomplish. But retirement does not necessarily mean a loss of identity; a key task in retiring is to reassess your identity and, if necessary, sculpt a new one. You may recognise that while there is loss, at the same time there are many opportunities to develop new roles and identities. There are many examples of people making successful transitions, often without any concept of a job to redefine them or to demonstrate their worth. They do it through developing new communities, immersing themselves in their interests and in activities, or picking up strands of their earlier life.

While not glossing over the difficulties, or assuming that we can control or predict all that life will throw at us, we believe that thinking ahead can help you realise your hopes and dreams, and can open up your lives to the possibilities before you. The period of retirement for many, many people is the 'time of their lives'.

Be challenged and stimulated by your retirement. It won't always be easy but hold your nerve, take risks, surprise yourself, do things, try new stuff, experiment, be bold, be brave and have lots of laughs along the way.

Chapter 1

Retirement Ain't What It Used to Be

Once upon a time retirement was predictable. You left work on your 65th birthday (or whatever date your employer decided), received a gold watch and walked off into a life of golf and grandchildren. We call this old model 'walking off a cliff'.

Retirement has changed in the last decade. Nowadays you retire at a time you decide and, instead of an abrupt departure, it is increasingly likely that you will chose to reduce your hours gradually. And life after work is likely to involve a wide range of activities – including golf and grandchildren if that is for you, but also many other things, especially if you don't play golf and don't have grandchildren. What is more, your retirement is likely to last for 20 years or more. In this new version it is possible to tailor decisions to suit individual circumstances and wishes.

The implications of this new version of retirement go far beyond the effects on pensions. They include deciding about when and how to retire, preparing for a longer period of life in retirement, and considering the impact of these decisions upon all aspects of life, including relationships with those closest to you. Here we look at the wider picture, setting the context for a more detailed exploration of retirement choices and opportunities.

What Is Changing?

Retirement is changing and the implications for people's lives are enormous and affect everyone. Governments in the UK and other countries have already altered policies that affect older workers and their pensions. Employers need to adjust their approaches to older workers. Those who provide services specifically tailored to the needs of older people (e.g., pensions, health services, care, as well as entertainment, holidays, accommodation and specialist equipment) will have to review what is on offer.

What is changing? For a start, many of us are living longer. News released in December 2012 that over 10 million people alive today can expect to live to 100 startled and disconcerted many of us. Two million of them are already over 50 years old. Currently about 12 million people in the UK are retired, and this will increase to 15 million by 2030. 'Many millions of us will be spending around a third of our lives or more in retirement in the future,' said Steve Webb, minister for pensions, making the important connection between increased longevity and retirement. The significant change to later life – that more of us are living longer – seems to have crept up while we were busy working. Life expectancy in the 20th century has steadily increased. Boys born in 1901 in the UK could expect to live to the age of 49 and girls to 50. Those born after the second world war could expect to live a further 20 years, to 69 for men and 70 for women. Today, men and women of 65 can expect to live for another 17–19 years (until they are 82 and 84) in retirement. This is a long time to be retired.

During the same time that life expectancy has risen so dramatically, the significance of pensions and retirement has been transformed. State pensions were first introduced in the UK in 1909 for a small number of men and women over 70, with means of less than £31.10, who had previously been in employment. They were designed to 'lift the shadow of the workhouse from the homes of the poor', according to David Lloyd George, the chancellor who introduced the reform. When a limited contributory scheme was introduced in 1925 and extended to everyone in the 1946 National Insurance Act, there was no expectation of supporting people for 17–19 years. The original calculations behind the introduction of state, work-related and private pensions have been put under pressure by longer and healthier lives. Saving for the future has always been a strategy for those with both affluence and prudence. Now, retirement for most people is no longer a short period of time before their death.

The situation for women in retirement has also been changing. In the last 30 years women have made up an increasing proportion of the labour market. They have seen the pay gap narrow, the idea that their place is in the home eroded, and inroads made into the male-dominated sectors. By 2008 about two-thirds of women were in employment, with little difference between those who were married (64 per cent) and unmarried (62 per cent), and making up 45 per cent of the workforce. Patterns of work have changed so that women have entered the job market in increasing numbers, especially in part-time work, and at the same time traditionally male full-time work in industries such as coal mining, steel works and car assembly has dramatically declined. The labour market has seen an increase in flexible and less well-paid work in services and the knowledge economy. These changes have affected both men's and women's employment.

Women suffer from inequalities accrued from work breaks, returning to work part-time and at a lower level than previously. Consequently, they are often in a disadvantaged position in relation to their pensions. Government reforms are addressing some inequalities by introducing a flat-rate state pension for everyone.

There are three further factors that bear upon the retirement landscape, which reinforce the idea that 'retirement ain't what it used to be'. The first is the growing cost for the economy of supporting more people for longer. The increased call upon pension funds has been anticipated for some time. But the second factor is the unfortunate concurrence of this demand with an economic recession.

The government's response has been to encourage people to stay in work for longer, by progressively raising the state pension age (SPA), abolishing the default retirement age (DRA) and requiring employers to make pension contributions (Pensions Act 2011). Public sector pensions are being changed so that future payments decrease, while contributions increase. In addition, many pension schemes are likely to be changed to provide payments based not on final salaries but on average salaries. The reduction in the value of pensions may be as much as a third according to a 2013 Pensions Policy Institute analysis, and it is therefore unsurprising that public sector workers have made clear their disapproval of these changes. Less generous and delayed pension payments will affect retirement decisions for many people.

The decrease in the size of the working population is the final factor of the changing landscape. Employers will increasingly need to turn to older workers to fill the resulting skills gap. Alongside the increased life expectancy, the birth rate has fluctuated. At the start of this century it reached a low point and it has been rising since. While the proportion of the population aged 15–64 has remained stable over the last hundred years (around 65 per cent), the 0–14s have almost reduced by half (from 31 per cent in 1911 to 18 per cent in 2011). The proportion of people aged 65 and over has trebled, from 5 per cent in 1911 to 16 per cent in 2011. A skills shortage is already being created as people retire and fewer younger people join the workforce.

Increasing numbers of older workers are staying in employment for longer, frequently in part-time positions, with some choosing to work until they die. While some fear that this will deprive younger people of promotion opportunities, there are others who suggest that older people's active and longer economic participation will benefit the economy through prolonging people's involvement in active economic life.

The 'demographic time bomb' is the media's term for these changes. This negative and violent image suggests that drastic measures are required, and it is usually accompanied by an assumption that older people drain national resources, and that retired people are dependent or 'a negative burden on the state', as former benefits chief Lord Bichard put it in 2012. This viewpoint suggests that pensioners are in a similar position as other benefit recipients, ignoring the contributions they have already made through national insurance. In Lord Bichard's opinion, people receiving the state pension might be required to 'earn' their benefits by voluntary activities or part-time work. He asked: 'Are we using all the incentives at our disposal to encourage older people not just to be a negative burden on the state but actually be a positive part of society?' Lord Bichard hasn't done his homework. A better image of older people would be as a valued resource. 'Older people ... are the solution to many of the challenges facing the UK, not the problem,' according to Phillip Blond, director of the ResPublica thinktank. He puts it down to 'their experience, sense of community and civic engagement'.

Put all of this together and the picture includes more people who are 65 or older living for longer. They are being encouraged to remain in work for longer, and will be increasingly able to choose how and when they leave work. They are better educated than previous generations, and they also expect more from life and frequently more from themselves.

The contrast of this new situation with the old model is stark. Many people still refer to retirement age as 60 or 65, as they have been planning towards it throughout their working lives. It has become a default position, despite the fact that there is no retirement age now. The new version of retirement has more flexibility and variation, no longer the one-size-fits-all version. It brings with it possibilities, opportunities and a healthy dose of ambivalence for most retirees.

So What Is Retirement?

The very word 'retirement' is imprecise. It carries in its meaning what is not, or what has been left behind. In everyday use it means ending work, which is frequently an inaccurate picture. And it implies a lack of activity, which is again frequently not the case. The French *prendre la retraite* (literally to take the retreat) can be associated with ideas of military or spiritual withdrawal. Active retirees may find it hard to associate themselves with a description of their lives as 'withdrawal' or to respond positively to enquiries such as 'What are you going to do with your time?' In our case we both put in place activities that included fee-paid consultancy work, as well as freelance writing, voluntary activities and plans to spend time on other interests.

In the new world, retirement is becoming more loosely coupled with age and pensions. It is becoming less associated with giving up working. So what does retirement mean?

Retirement used to refer to an event: giving up work. The new version is better described as a series of transitions. There may be defining moments, as there was for the man who described his experience to Caroline as shocking and abrupt: 'One day I was working and the next day I wasn't.' People can sometimes talk about a date when they retire, and this is often marked by a celebration event, and by drawing a pension. But, increasingly, people are taking a more graduated approach to the end of their working life. For example, we both ended our contracts (retired) but continued (after the required break) to be employed on a more flexible basis doing some of the same work, as well as undertaking paid work for other organisations.

The close association between leaving employment and receiving a pension is also outdated, but it is common in everyday use, especially in the media. Many people, it seems, see retirement as synonymous with receiving their pension. The coverage of the SPA being raised demonstrates this everyday association: 'The government speeds up plans to raise the retirement age' (*Daily Mail*). For many, however, it is not one and the same to end work and get a pension. For example, it is possible to receive a pension while continuing to work, and some pension schemes allow for a partial fund withdrawal while people continue to work on a part-time basis, in a kind of top-up arrangement. The association of retiring from work with drawing pensions has become looser and is now more controlled by the individual.

The most widespread use of the word 'retirement' draws on financial assumptions. In this definition a retired person is one who is no longer employed, not working for money. Physicist Richard Harris challenged this definition when he returned to work at 68 as a consultant for a defence company's Trusted Experts scheme. His motivation was not financial. 'I want to work and my employers want me to work,' he told *Saga* magazine in May 2010, 'and it puts me back in control of my retirement.' He described himself as simultaneously working and retired.

Using 'retirement' to describe a person's economic status can therefore be inaccurate. A retired person can be moving in and out of employment. It is not a settled state for many people and does not capture the experience of retirement as a series of transitions.

So the word 'retirement' is subject to different meanings, depending on the context and the user's assumptions. To describe a person as retired may be acceptable to some but not to others in similar circumstances.

Yet another version is based on psychological assumptions, where individuals define retirement for themselves. Our own difficulties in responding to enquiries about what we would do with our time arose from not defining ourselves as retired in the sense of no longer working. Indeed to write this, we are doing what we frequently did during our careers – sitting at our laptops, writing for publication and contributing to our incomes.

It is more constructive to use 'retirement' to refer to a series of changes that form the overall process of transition, which results in gradual or one-step withdrawal from paid work. The idea of *morphing* captures something of the gradual transition from one relationship between life and work to another. There is also a distinction between *retiring* (the process of moving towards the end of a phase in which life is defined by work) and *retirement* (the experience of being in this new phase).

So there are many overlapping meanings, yet none of them on their own capture the full flexibility and gradualness of the transitions. Because it is a series of transitions, retirement requires adjustment over time – from anticipation and planning, during the period of withdrawing from work (which may be brief or drawn out), and afterwards when people see themselves as retired. Eileen initially referred to herself as a 'retired academic now working as a freelance writer'. She has now dropped the first part of this description. In this book we have retained the term 'retirement' as it is in universal use, but wish for a more appropriate phrase.

Retirement as a Series of Transitions

It can be helpful to think of the overall transition into retirement as passing through a series of overlapping zones or stages:

Zone	Activities and states of mind	Issues
Zone 1: Just looking	Awareness of retirement as a career stage	What will this mean?
Zone 2: Preparations	Researching approaches to retirement, and possible ways forward Ambivalence Apprehension Excitement Researching Planning Preparation	Assessing reasons to leave work or to stay Anticipating effects of changing work patterns on life When to go? How to go?
Zone 3: Retiring	Planning Preparation Decisions Ambiguity	Making some changes – for example, reducing hours in stages, bridging job Future with less or no work
Zone 4: Novice in retirement	Monitoring Reviewing Adjusting plans	Reflection on effects of decisions and other factors on preferred retirement situation Emotions about leaving work
Zone 5: Veteran in retirement	Satisfied with the transitions made Enjoying the time of their life	Still reflecting and learning

The five zones are designed to encourage you to think about your retirement in relation to your life, and to help you predict and understand the actions, issues and states of mind implicated in your decisions. The pace and timing by which any individual moves through the zones will vary considerably, and a few people will be catapulted into Zone 3 without the benefit of preparations – in other words, people are still falling off cliffs. Also, of course, not everyone survives to experience veteran status. Many people are felled by ill health or accidents on the way, or blown off course by other outside influences. While the trend is for individuals to be required to make more decisions about retirement, there are many factors beyond their control that can change their outcomes:

Scenario	Possible factors
Happy and keen to retire	Favourable financial situation Looking forward to doing other things Worked for long enough Work no longer enjoyable
Forced or felt forced to retire	At or beyond common retirement age Early retirement imposed, by health or redundancy
Don't want to retire	Still enjoying work Afraid of retirement
Blown off course	Family circumstances affect decision Individual's health influences retirement age Employer's policies overrule preference

The manner in which people retire influences their responses to the changes, as the following examples show.

Lorna Hoey, a former teacher, told us that she doesn't miss all the things she's done, the schools she's worked in, the projects she's been involved in, the clever, funny, inspiring pupils and colleagues that she's known. She was very clear that although she had loved teaching, 'it's time to move on'.

By contrast, John White, a postman, who was forced to retire at 69 (before the DRA was withdrawn) said: 'This felt like I was being sacked.' He didn't want to retire.

Marianne Coleman, a university lecturer, was also enjoying her work as she approached the age when she could consider retiring. Typical of the third scenario, and like many women of her generation who had a previous career break in order to raise children, she was at the peak of her career. 'If like me, you feel your job is worthwhile, interesting, satisfying and crucial to your identity, it seems perverse to give it up, and retirement may seem threatening.'

Finally, Gil Bennet's experience fits the scenario of being 'blown off course'. She was forced to leave abruptly her career as a deputy head teacher of a secondary school in the north of England as a result of poor health. This led to a period of depression for her, before she could find her way to a better life.

Retirement is still one of the most important and potentially difficult transitions in people's lives, despite – or even because of – all the changes described above. Choices have increased, and so has the pressure for decisions to be made by the individuals themselves. The old model – being required to leave paid work at 65 – is not always very helpful in providing solutions to the challenges faced or in answering today's retirees' questions. A key factor in making the transition successfully is to regard retirement as an opportunity to do things without the restrictions imposed by work, rather than as the end of an active life.

Retirement Choices Are About More than Pensions

Retirement changes all aspects of your life, not just your income. Your relationship with money, time, immediate family, social connections, health and purpose in life will all be affected. Some things change immediately, like the pattern of your week and your income. Others can take many months or even years of adjustment.

You lose a work-focused identity and develop a new one based on other activities. It may continue to change as you move from novice to veteran retiree.

Your quality of life is influenced by the availability of particular resources. In a 2005 research report, James Nazroo found six contributing factors to the quality of life at an older age (listed here in order of importance):

1. support networks, including quality of neighbourhood: social, emotional and practical;
2. material conditions: income, wealth and housing;
3. health;
4. having free time;
5. having a role; and
6. independence, not having to rely on others.

When you consider your situation in light of these six factors, it will be clear that there are some things that you can change and some that you cannot. And it may be possible to plan ahead and prepare for some of them.

These resources are not unrelated – for example, health and the ability to be independent are closely connected. Your changing relationships, with money or with your partner for example, do not happen in isolation. They are interconnected. The state of your health can affect the quality of your life, but health itself is affected by feelings of purposefulness and social connections. Activity in pursuit of your interests can lead you into productive social relations. And so on.

All changes bring ambivalent feelings. Some things you might want to lose (an uncomfortable journey to work perhaps), or you might find yourself dreading the loss of that same thing (a journey that provides time to pursue private activities, such as reading, or an opportunity for exercise if you walk to work). In the pre-retirement zone, when all aspects of retirement are being contemplated and little is clear, ambiguity is likely to be at its most contradictory. There will always be ambivalence in the face of the gains and losses of all of life's transitions.

Images evoking retiring, such as a door, an airlock, 'going over to the other side', 'being released into the wild', 'beginning a new chapter', as well as the more painful 'falling off a cliff', all imply movement from one state to another. Some of these images imply an easier passage than others. The ways in which you describe the anticipated changes, the images you hold in your mind, may tell you something about your attitudes to retirement.

As you approach these complex changes, thinking ahead can help avoid or modify some problems, prepare the way for an enriched life and make a significant contribution to your well-being. Through all the stages of retirement, choices can be made and new challenges faced. While the scope of the anticipated changes may be enormous, it's worth remembering that not everything changes at the same time and you can therefore afford to take small steps. Few decisions are irrevocable, however large.

Reminders:

- Think ahead. You can't prepare for everything, you can't anticipate everything, but you can plan and work towards your preferred choices.
- Small steps may be more effective than grand gestures.
- Few decisions are irrevocable.

Your well-being will derive from some new sources. The significance of factors that contribute to the quality of your life will vary from another person's and, moreover, such factors are often not within your control. Ensuring you have all the necessary support is an important part of the preparation.

Closing Thoughts

Marianne Coleman expressed the fear she felt before retiring, saying, 'I used to think that retiring meant going through a door, and on the other side it was the end.' Fears about retirement being the final stage, however, are in part inherited from the old ideas of retirement. But for Marianne these initial concerns did not match the reality. She is still actively involved in research and writing, but has also found pleasure in caring for her grandchildren and an older family member, taking up a new sport and travelling with her husband. She is a great role model.

In this new retirement era, there are more resources and choices available than for previous generations, such as better education and more disposable income. Many retirees expect to be fully involved in the pleasures of life. This can be expressed as being able to make a contribution for longer.

Expect more of life and of yourself. Plan to achieve more, realise your dreams, experience more of the world and create the best life that you can.

Chapter 2

On Not Falling off a Cliff: Decisions about Leaving Employment

In Shakespeare's *King Lear*, a single action triggers tragedy. The old king gives up his kingdom, an act that leads to warfare and family division, as well as his own descent into turmoil and madness. Lear's purpose was 'to shake all cares and business from our age', to allow him an 'unburdened crawl towards death'. Lear did not consider the cruelty of others nor the consequences to his own sense of self, and this neglect led to the tragedy that unfolded. *King Lear* was written over 400 years ago and, like so much of Shakespeare, still has relevance today.

The image of retirement as a cliff, over which a retiree is in danger of falling, is one of the most commonly used, and it is an abrupt and painful image. It is ironic that the blinded Gloucester, the other old man in *King Lear*, is led to a fictitious cliff by his disguised son Edgar, planning to jump and end his life. His suicide bid is thwarted, and he lives to die later of a bursting heart.

The falling-off-a-cliff approach to retirement has its roots in an outdated model from the time when people left work at 65. There was little preparation and perhaps a small celebration, a gold watch moment. Ted retired from his work in local government in the 1980s. When we interviewed him, he told us:

> I had no choice about when to retire. You went on your 65th birthday. There was no preparation to speak of. The accounts office asked you to come and see them and sort out your pension. On the day, I had a meeting with some colleagues in the afternoon and then I left.

In a break from the past, two connected choices now dominate decisions about ending work: first, when to go and, second, how to go (in stages or in one leap). It is now the individual who decides when employment will end because a fixed retirement age is no longer legal. However, choice about leaving employment is constrained by circumstances, not a matter of whim or simple preference, and some circumstances will ensure that there is no choice to speak of.

The Big Decision

There are many good reasons for retiring: no longer enjoying work, not wanting to learn required skills and knowledge, wanting an easier life, wanting to do something different, wanting to do nothing. Other things being equal, it would be foolish not to finish working in these situations. But other things have a habit of not being equal, and this is true in retirement. Money is one of the first things that may make it difficult to choose when and how to retire. Another is that people often feel ambivalent – you may have the financial means to give up work but do not want to stop working, at least not yet. Retiring changes a great deal more than your financial situation and how you spend your time, as Lear discovered. Competing and contradictory factors make it a difficult decision that requires plenty of forethought. There is no road map to retirement.

Ambivalence can cloud the issues. While feeling positive about some changes that retirement will bring, fears about what will be lost can simultaneously loom large. You work in order to earn money, but work also fulfils other functions. It provides an identity, a social environment, a structure for your time and, maybe, a sense of purpose – often described as 'making a contribution'. You have to face finding a new identity, and replacing the connections and sense of purpose – 'a reason to get up in the morning'. Thinking and planning ahead makes sense, even if you are fortunate enough to face these changes with confidence.

And it's not just what retirement will bring that needs to be considered. There may be things to lose that make the prospect of leaving difficult. In a survey carried out by Ipsos MORI in 2008, 63 per cent of workers aged over 55 said they stayed in work because of the money. They anticipated they would also miss the following when they retired:

- their work friends (67 per cent);
- the challenge of the work they do (53 per cent);
- office humour and gossip (42 per cent); as well as
- a reason to get out of the house (40 per cent).

In this list, losing the social and purposeful aspects of work looms large. The old version of retirement is of economic and social redundancy. If you hold this image in your head, then leaving work will appear very intimidating.

Lear wanted to keep his identity as king, but not the 'cares and business' of kingship. One of the arguments between Lear and his older daughters was that he wished to retain his title and retinue. In doing this he compromises his own ability to unburden his journey towards death. Before the action of the play is over, Lear recognises that he has become 'a poor, infirm, weak, and despised old man'. It is not uncommon for people to find it difficult to face the question 'What will I be when I am no longer a butcher, a baker, a candlestick maker or a king?' Think about how you see and define yourself in the future and how others might see and define you. Holding on to your old identity is not a good strategy for adapting to change.

There is no road map to retirement today because it's rarely a single event, rather it is a series of transitions. There may be a moment, such as a retirement party, when a person is recognised as having given up work. But, frequently, people move more gradually into the status of retiree. The effect of the decision to leave employment in one step, or in stages, will resonate through life and will also affect family and friends, sometimes for several years. Here are the factors to consider.

Work-Related Factors

One of the most important factors is how you feel about work. Here's a quick task – decide which one of these statements best describes your attitude to your current work situation:

1. I love work and can't imagine not doing it.
2. I enjoy work now but I'll be ready to give it up soon.
3. I enjoy work but it's becoming harder to keep up with new practices.
4. I used to enjoy work but it's changed too much.
5. It's the right time for me to stop.
6. I hate work and can't wait to finish.

Now, a few questions.

What factors came to mind when you selected one response? It is likely that the task raised ambivalent feelings, things you want to lose and gain, things you don't want to lose or gain. Ambivalence is common and talking about these feelings with friends or colleagues may clarify this.

If No 1 applies to you, then why not stay put? There may be no reason for you to retire. So why are you reading this book? Perhaps you want to go on working, but with some changes such as reducing your hours?

If No 2 applies, then you may want to start thinking about what your options are. Start preparing: talk to people, look out for a retiring course, start thinking about your finances. It's never too early to make enquiries and preparations.

If Nos 3 or 4 apply, you might want to get support to refresh your skills or knowledge. Your response may not be a reason to leave your work. If you don't want to learn new skills or go on a refresher course, then perhaps it is time to give up work. Think about what appeals to you in making this decision.

If you said yes to Nos 5 or 6, you are clear it's time to act. Announce you are ready to retire. Will this surprise people – your boss, your family, your friends? Check your plans.

Philip Roth, the American author, surprised many when he announced he was ready to retire. In 2012 he told a *New Yorker* interviewer:

> When I finished I decided to reread all of my books beginning with the last, *Nemesis*. I wanted to see if I had wasted my time writing. And I thought it was more or less a success. At the end of his life, the boxer Joe Louis said, 'I did the best I could with what I had'. It's exactly what I would say of my work: I did the best I could with what I had. After that, I decided I was finished with fiction. I don't want to read it, I don't want to write it, and I don't even want to talk about it anymore. I dedicated my life to the novel. I studied them, I taught them, I wrote them, and I read them. At the exclusion of nearly everything else. It's enough!

If it's enough – stop.

Your attitude to your current work will help you decide about when and how you retire. You will need to decide whether you take some time to leave (e.g., work part-time or reduce your hours) or take immediate action and stop working straight away.

You may decide to continue working for the time being, but want to modify your working conditions. The Trades Union Congress (TUC) produced the 'Managing Age' guide, directed at employers and trade unions, on the employment of older workers. It suggests six questions for older employees to consider:

1.   What kind of work do you want to do?
2.   Do you want to change your hours?
3.   Can you share your knowledge with colleagues?
4.   How long do you want to work?
5.   What are the financial implications?
6.   What are the pension implications?

Some pension schemes allow for flexibility in later years. You may want to continue with the work you are doing, or you may want to try something new, or adjust your hours and responsibility. Some pension schemes allow you to delay drawing your pension; others allow employees to continue in part-time work after reaching pension age, while claiming some of the pension at the same time. Research this with your pension provider, consult a financial adviser and make proposals to your employer.

Flexible working is becoming more common, according to the TUC. The coalition government is committed to extending the statutory right to all employees to request flexible working. It currently applies only to parents and carers. These arrangements can benefit employers as well as employees, which accounts for its increase. It also fits the government's policies to keep people in work for longer.

Another way of making a transition from regular employment to retirement can be through offering your services on a freelance basis. There are many attractions in this arrangement. You remain in control of how much work you undertake, while you continue to use your expertise, skills and reputation. It is possible to earn good money, to keep your hand in, to maintain and make new contacts.

Beware of three false messages that float around, in casual conversation, in the media, with friends. These might influence your thinking about leaving or staying. The first false message is that there is a normal retirement age that should guide decisions about when to retire. This message says that everyone should retire around 65. The old model of retirement is influential here, one that links ending work to a birthdate, as was the case for Ted quoted above. Also influential is the close association of pensions, and especially the SPA, with retirement. The separation of retirement and pensions in the new version of retirement was discussed in the previous chapter. Many variations are possible. You can work and take your state pension, you can retire and not draw any pension (although this is probably rare), or you can work a bit and take your pension a bit and continue contributing to your pension all at the same time. But the idea of a fixed retirement age remains strong in the minds of those who are closest to 65, possibly because they have been planning for that moment for several years.

Here's the second false idea. Older workers should make way for younger people. The 'should' in that sentence implies a duty or responsibility. It implies the right of a younger person over an older person to promotion. It is a form of ageism. Older workers have experience, knowledge and wisdom that employers should not waste. It's also a false idea because a skills gap is already opening up in the employment market. There are too few younger workers to fill the spaces of those who are leaving employment. The economy needs older workers.

The third false idea is the common belief that older people have a reduced capacity to work, that they can't hack it any more. This is another form of ageism and, like all prejudice, has no basis in reality. Age is not a strong determinant of reduced capacity, the Health and Safety Executive tells us. The Equality Act of 2010 made age discrimination illegal. This false idea persists despite many people who keep going well beyond any normal retirement age: bishops, members of the House of Lords, politicians, actors, writers, painters, architects, mature students, newspaper owners, butchers, bakers and monarchs.

The amount of overt age discrimination is decreasing, but it is still possible to find employers resisting the necessary adaptations for their ageing workforce. And older workers might find themselves made redundant (e.g., through restructuring or downsizing), and then being unable to gain new employment. John had been made redundant from the accounts department in a company that folded recently. He told us that as he was 62 he was afraid he would only be able to get jobs on very low pay, like collecting trolleys in a supermarket or washing cars. 'It's so degrading,' he admitted.

In effect, some older workers have been retired. It is especially hard for those who become unemployed or are forced to live on incapacity benefit and who have failed to find alternative employment. For these older workers age discrimination is experienced as poor employment prospects.

Employers' responsibilities towards employees have increased, we believe, as a result of ending the fixed retirement age. Even in 2011 nearly two-thirds of the 11.2 million people aged between 50 and 64 were in employment. Paying attention to the ageing workforce is a significant issue for employers.

Health-Related Factors

Health and physical condition are also significant factors in deciding when to retire. For some, the opportunity to spend time on improving their physical health is an important encouragement to retire. But many 65-year-olds are fit and able to work. Sashi Patel had run his own newsagent business before he retired, but at 66 he became bored and decided to take employment at Asda. Far from finding this work degrading, Sashi enjoys still making a contribution:

> My job keeps me fit and full of energy – and it gives me a reason to get up and out of the house each day … I like to feel that I am contributing something and as long as I can keep working, I will do.

Julia, a medical receptionist, told us that she was not planning to retire at 65. She was enjoying her work and said, 'Just because you turn 65 doesn't mean you're not fit enough to carry on.'

Some work is more physically demanding and some bodies are less able to sustain the physical demands of work. For these people one answer is to leave work, but other options are to seek adaptions to the work, or to the hours, or even to the place where work is carried out. It is regrettable to be forced into ending employment by ill health. If this applies to you, try investigating the feasible alternatives with your employer.

Finance-Related Factors

Financial considerations obviously dominate and, knowing this, governments use alterations to pensions to exert pressure on individuals to stay longer at work. And, according to investment banks and pension fund organisations, many people are already responding by delaying their retirement or putting off any plans to retire at all. Indeed, the number of people in employment aged 65 and over has reached 900,000 – the highest figure since comparable records began. Approximately one-third of this number are part-time workers. This is the only group for which the employment rate has risen since 2008.

People fall into four categories in the face of financial changes: ostriches, sleepwalkers, rabbits or wise planners. The burying-its-head-in-the-sand stance of the ostrich is not tenable because: it is uncomfortable (the truth being avoided is still the truth, even if it is unknown); it is unrealistic (as before, the reality is still there); and eventually even an ostrich comes up for air (and has to face the figures that may have got worse while its head was buried). It is not rational or comfortable, but, in the face of fears about income in retirement, there are people whose strategy is to delay finding the truth.

Sleepwalkers are the millions of people, within a decade of their state pension, who have still not thought about how long they might live in retirement. Over half of individuals aged 50–64 and not yet retired have never thought about how many years they will need to fund. Typically, women underestimate by four years and men by two years. Sleepwalkers are not usually good decision-makers.

Then there are the rabbits, transfixed in the headlights by the reduction in pension entitlements and the raising of the SPA. Rabbits are famous for multiplying, and this what they have done since the changes were introduced. In 2010 half of the working population said that they don't know when they will retire – if ever (up from 1 per cent in 2008). And 10 per cent have no plans to retire (with the DRA, everybody had plans in 2008).

Some rabbits react to pension changes by suspending their plans to stop working. There are 3.5 million of these people. Others respond by planning to delay their departure from work – many until they are 65 (2.3 million – up from 1.9 million in 2009), and a sizeable group (100,000) until they are 76. The trend to delay retirement is likely to continue, as levels of uncertainty about pension income increase across the population.

Another group of rabbits have responded by making no financial provision – perhaps as much as a fifth of all workers. Perhaps they are unable to set aside the recommended equivalent of 12 per cent of their salary: many women, people in low-paid work or those who have been unemployed for any significant time, as well as those who started late in making their pension contribution. Only 38 per cent of women (compared with 60 per cent of men) are saving adequately. Altogether, 48 per cent of people do not save enough for their pensions according to Scottish Widows.

The wise financiers, on the other hand, are equipped with knowledge and they monitor their situation, checking periodically the value of pensions, investments and changes to entitlements (such as the frequently changing rules about the SPA). Pensions are not very interesting, especially when you are in work. Financial advisers are an invaluable support for those people who want someone else to take an interest in their pension and their financial prospects in retirement, rabbits and all. Wise planners will also benefit from their knowledge.

Well, how would you describe yourself? Are you an ostrich, a sleepwalker, a rabbit or a wise planner? In which category would you like to be? It's never too late, or too early, to seek professional financial advice to help you become a wise planner.

Family-Related Factors

One person's decision to retire can affect many other people who are close to them: their partner, other family members and/or close community members. The impact on your partner may be an obvious factor, but there may be a wider impact that needs to be considered, such as on groups and activities that have developed close to your place of work. These may not be predictable. One of the unexplored areas, for example, is the assumption that others may make about your increased availability.

Replacing work with the care of children or the demands of elder care can be the exchange of one set of burdens for another. Angela's story reveals a complicated confusion of duty and exploitation:

> I retired at the end of April when I was 60. In June my mother fell and broke her leg and I went down from Manchester, where I live with my husband and our two grown-up children, to Cornwall to look after her. She was frustrated that she couldn't get around like she used to as [she] had been very active since my father died ten years earlier. I didn't find it easy to be around her as she was cross and critical a lot of the time. In August Jim, my husband, rented a nearby holiday cottage as my mother couldn't bear to have him and the two girls all staying in the house. She said that would upset her as it would be noisy and crowded. I decided to stay one night with my family and the next night with my mother and so on. When I was not with my mother, the neighbour, who was good and very kind, popped in to make sure everything was all right.
>
> The problem with this arrangement was that when I returned to Mum's she would be very difficult and was even more critical and controlling. The same arrangement was made for Christmas. I never went home to Manchester as I felt it

would take too long to get back in case of an emergency. Gradually she began to get confused and this made matters worse. Jim suggested that Mum needed professional care and looked around for care homes in Manchester. But Mum was very upset when we talked to her about it and refused to move and became very tearful. I couldn't bear it. I felt I could not please my mother or my husband. It's hard thinking about the best thing to do. At the moment I'm still with my mother in Cornwall but I miss Jim so much. I am hoping he will retire soon. He has a small company and I don't think he wants to give that up and he likes living in the city. This is not the retirement I imagined. I feel trapped and looking after Mum is exhausting physically and emotionally.

Not all experiences of caring for older relatives are as anguished as Angela's. However, her story demonstrates some important points. It is often women who are called upon or feel called upon to undertake family care. For Angela there is a toxic mix: a mother-daughter relationship that is increasingly demanding at the expense of her marriage, exacerbated by travel between Manchester and Cornwall; a mother whose worsening health makes the care more difficult, especially as she resists the need for professional care. No wonder Angela feels trapped, disappointed and exhausted.

Undertaking care of both older and younger relatives has implications for deciding about when and how to retire. And these implications may not make the decision any easier. Carers who have not yet left work are already considering the demands that caring makes on their working situation, and they are increasingly requesting more flexible work arrangements from employers. However, an NHS survey in 2010 showed that many eligible workers were unaware of the right to request flexible working. It has also been reported that about a quarter of those who are in work and acting as carers may not be getting the benefits to which they are entitled.

The burden of care is more likely to fall upon women than men (60 per cent of carers are women). The impact of this care is not limited to the time spent providing the care itself. Working flexible hours often means fewer hours and for lower pay. And women on low incomes are more likely to give up work or reduce their hours in order to care for grandchildren. The NHS survey found that care responsibilities affected many people's ability to be active in the employment market. A Carers UK survey found that families reported losing an average of £11,000 a year in earnings. The benefit to the public purse is huge as carers bear the burden, but the personal price can be enormous, especially for those members of the 'sandwich generation' who are caring for both older and young family members.

Caring for a sick, disabled or elderly family member can have many rewards, and indeed many people welcome the opportunity to spend more time with ageing parents while they can. But it can also be very stressful, as Angela found. It is especially demanding to care for those suffering from dementia, or those who are very frail and ill. The demands can be unpredictable and accelerate without warning. It seems that it is especially stressful if the carer is edging towards an important decision, such as when their dependant may require more professional care or may need to be admitted to a home. Not surprisingly, 52 per cent of carers have suffered from stress, and carers are twice as likely to become ill or develop a disability themselves. And, at its most difficult, it can be an isolating experience.

Both psychological and physical health problems can result from caring, either from the worry or the physical strain. Some 40 per cent of carers have significantly high distress and depression levels; older carers who report physical strain have a 63 per cent higher likelihood of death over a four-year period. Cases such as the one below by Julie Fearn have led GPs to suggest that carers should be routinely screened for depression. Her story, reported on the BBC News website in May

2013, shows how debilitating it can be to be thrown into the role of a primary carer:

> My husband was diagnosed with terminal cancer shortly after we retired. I have been caring for him for 18 months. His diagnosis was a massive blow to our retirement plans. Our life has reduced considerably and the emotional strain is tremendous. We used to have a social life and go on holiday. Now we just stay in the house most of the time.
>
> I'm his primary carer, but I'm not medically trained, yet I'm meant to inform the hospital if his health deteriorates rapidly. This creates a huge sense of responsibility for me.
>
> I have a network of friends and family, but still suffer from anxiety and depression and take medication. It was a few months though before I went to the GP for help. The problem is, unless you bring your depression to the attention of the GP, no one will do anything to help.
>
> Screening is really important. There should be a referral system so that when a person is diagnosed with an illness, people caring for the person have an appointment with the doctor to check how they are coping.

And yet, despite the huge strain, so many older people are caring for others. The 2001 census showed that more people in their 50s than in any other age group are unpaid carers – about one-fifth of this age group. If they are already caring for family members and they are in their 50s, this will be a factor in them deciding about whether to continue in paid employment.

The NHS survey reported that about 5 million adults look after disabled, sick or elderly people. A quarter of these are aged over 65 (see table), and 27 per cent of all carers described themselves as retired. These 'retired' carers challenge all assumptions about dependent and inactive retirees.

Age	Per cent of carers
16–34	18
35–44	15
45–54	21
55–64	21
65+	25

Fifty-four per cent of the people who took on caring responsibilities said they felt it was expected of them, as 'it's what families do'. Fifty-three per cent said they made a willing choice themselves to help out. A small minority of 7 per cent said they had the time to care for others because they were not working.

Looking after children is another aspect of care that often falls upon older family members. This is partly a result of changing patterns of work for women: the proportion of mothers in the work-force has increased dramatically in the last few decades. It is often the grandparents who step in to provide childcare, especially for less well-off parents who find the cost of formal care prohibitively expensive. Many families would not manage easily without the help of grandparents. There are 7 million grandparents in the UK and half of them help out with childcare, mostly unpaid. Their input is worth £33bn per annum.

'There are a lot of us around, if you look,' says Jennifer Evans in *Retiring Lives*.

> They pick up kids from school, look after them in the holidays, and generally enjoy that special relationship that means you can have fun without being ultimately responsible. I'm lucky to have six grandchildren living within about 500 metres of my house. Their age range is from 15 years to 15 months, so we do a variety of things together, in groups of two or three.

While it can be a very enjoyable aspect of being older, and perhaps of being retired, some grandparents risk hardship because by taking on childcare they can reduce their opportunities and energy for earning money. A small number of grandparents are paid for their time, but most do the work for nothing. Either way this can create tensions and the most common advice is to keep discussing with others what best suits you.

Influence from partners and other family considerations can also make a difference to your retirement plans. Sometimes one person can be pressurised to retire by the other in a partnership. This may explain an intriguing trend that people over 50 are more likely decide the same as their partner about whether to stay in work. Both parties must be sure of this next step. It is also intriguing that single people over 50 are less likely to be employed. The 2009 Economic & Labour Market Review that reported on these two trends sadly offered no explanations as to the reasons why.

There are advantages and disadvantages in not being in a relationship, living alone, not having children or grandchildren. Whatever retirement hopes and plans you have, your family circumstances will have an impact on them, so keep talking about and reviewing your situation.

Other Factors

The factors mentioned up to this point – work, family, physical or financial issues – may each encourage or dissuade you from giving up employment. Think about what else might be relevant to you. For example, retirement offers the opportunities to pursue interests and enthusiasms that you may have been putting off or curtailed during your working life. This may be the time you write your first novel, sail single-handed around the world, swim from Florida to Cuba, take up painting, learn a new language, improve your fitness, start up a new business, walk the length of Hadrian's Wall …

Staying on

If you chose the option of 'I love work and can't imagine not doing it', and if none of the other factors outweigh this choice, then don't retire. Charles Eugster, now 91, looked back at the late departure from his working life, saying in a *Guardian* feature:

> At 75, many of my friends began to pass away. People were getting older around me, but I was only just ready to retire. I carried on rowing and publishing a dentistry newsletter until I was 82.

The artist Bridget Riley is over 80 and still painting, the architect Richard Rogers is still working in his 80s and Diana Athill is still contributing to newspapers in her 90s. It is because they are successful or freelancing which enables them to go on working for as long as they able and want to. To achieve this flexibility, people considering retirement or wanting to return to work often look at taking up freelance work.

Marking the Occasion

People approaching retirement are assailed with advice about 'closure' through a retirement party. Take a moment to reflect whether closure and a party is what you want, or whether you are conforming to an established practice, despite or because of your own preferences. Some people want a party, with working colleagues from all phases of their career invited, speeches, reminiscences, embarrassing moments and all. Others want no such hoopla, only to slip away from work as if it were the end of a normal working day. One consideration is that your colleagues may like to have the occasion to thank you and say goodbye.

Caroline took the advice of David Wright in his poem 'Lines on Retirement, after Reading Lear' to avoid storms and retirement parties, while Eileen celebrated at a very enjoyable party, organised by a colleague and attended by people she had worked with over several decades. You choose.

Sadly, it seems from anecdotal evidence that arrangements for celebrating retirement are being individualised along with decisions about when and how to leave. For example, a colleague who retired after a distinguished career was asked to provide the drinks for her own leaving party. This is no way for an employer to pay tribute to the end of a career, even in straitened times.

Closing Thoughts

Many people's experience of retirement can be 'like walking off a cliff', especially if they make no preparations. After an active working life, some people may find the extreme contrast with the life they now live to be violent and painful. The image of falling off a cliff graphically captures the way some people are caught out, and find themselves like a cartoon caricature with their feet moving energetically as they always have, but gravity having its inevitable and painful effect.

This experience would be better if people made some preparations. Remember two things. One, it is always good to think ahead. Two, few decisions are once and for all. Decisions about retirement do not commit you forever. You can go and live abroad, and return to live again in the UK, and then start work again. You can set up a daily routine that mirrors a working day, but move to a more spontaneous way of living. You can retire and then go back to work.

As has been emphasised, there is no road map. Move gradually to avoid the cliff, anticipate a few important features and learn all the way.

Chapter 3

Not by Workers Alone: Employers and Workers' Retirement

A chapter that puts together employers with retirement? Employers just issue the P45 and say goodbye, don't they? On the contrary, the success or otherwise of your transition into retirement is strongly influenced by what your employers do. Employers can make older workers miserable by failing to recognise a desire for more training; or by treating workers who are about to retire as though they have already departed. But by providing information, access to courses and by supporting decision-making, employers can assist workers in the pre-retirement zone. By adjusting working conditions, employers can encourage longer working lives. They benefit from employing older workers, and with a shortage of younger people and skills, this need to support workers in their pre-retirement years will continue.

Employers' actions are significant in three areas:

- providing flexible working conditions for those who want to work for longer;
- supporting individual workers as they approach retirement; and
- retaining connections after work is finished.

41

Employers' actions in these areas affect workers' decisions about retirement. Many older workers would like to continue working, but not necessarily full-time or in the same work activity. And employers increasingly need to pay attention to older workers to ensure that their knowledge and experience are of benefit to the organisation. In short, employers' practices affect retirement choices.

You may be lucky enough to work in an organisation that provides flexible working conditions and support for retirees. However, a lot of people are disappointed by their employers' lack of concern or even lack of awareness. If you are in this position don't despair. There are several things you can do to encourage your employer to take note of your needs as you approach retirement. And you don't have to do this on your own. A major role of trade unions is to support older workers and negotiate with employers in order to ensure that your needs are met. You may be one of the 6 million workers in the UK, out of a workforce of 28 million, who belong to a trade union. See your union representative for advice and seek support for your retirement issues.

Staff associations and trade bodies such as the Confederation of British Industry and the Federation of Small Businesses have a role to play, too. Some are more active than others. But it's never too late to join. Your task is to ensure you act to get the support you need.

If you are self-employed, other forms of support are needed. Individuals can set up support groups or you can ask to join an existing one. A group of friends thinking about these issues may be a catalyst.

Employers and Older Workers

More and more people are working for longer. Sixty-two per cent of women and 59 per cent of men want to continue working beyond the state pension age (SPA). This figure came from a report published in 2010 by the Equality and Human Rights Commission called *Working Better: The Over-50s, the New Work Generation.* This trend of working beyond traditional retirement age will continue. Government policy is pushing workers this way by raising the SPA, changing public sector pension schemes and abolishing the employers' set retirement age (the default retirement age). The approaching skills shortage, together with the costs of supporting older citizens, are behind this policy.

Enlightened employers are encouraging this trend, fully aware of the benefits to their organisations. Older workers have skills and experience that can be passed on to others, especially through mentoring activities and knowledge management systems. Employment of older workers can address labour and skills shortages, as well as save money on recruitment and initial training. Retention of older workers boosts workplace morale, and increasing flexible work practices can assist with workforce planning. Retail and health services are accustomed to using flexible working as a way to match workforce levels with demand. Other occupations could benefit from such practices.

According to several reports, many older people want or need to work for longer, and employers must do more to adjust their attitudes and their practices. Strategies to retain older employees are presently non-existent, ad hoc or partial.

So what drives employers to improve arrangements for older workers? You would expect them to have the interests of their organisation uppermost in their minds. Indeed, as this extract from a Chartered Management Institute report shows, there are many benefits for an employer in retaining an ageing workforce:

> The desire to hold onto valuable knowledge and experience [of] older workers is by ... far the biggest driver for improving how older workers are managed, identified by ... 90 per cent of respondents. Experience is also implicit in the next two most popular ... drivers, the ability to mentor younger employees and skills shortages. It is clear ... that older employees are seen as valuable sources of knowledge ... Interestingly, the desire to reflect an ageing customer base –

an idea that is common in much of the diversity literature – is not widely regarded as important.

The report observed that managers recognise the importance of nurturing older workers' talent, but interestingly they don't always know how to do this effectively. So there is still work to be done in terms of training managers on how to deal with prospective retirees. As long ago as 2005, a Department for Work & Pensions review of research looking at extending working life in the UK identified six areas for development by employers and policy makers:

1. improving choice and control in the transition from work to retirement;
2. offering access to training and continuing education;
3. adopting a preventative approach to health issues;
4. ensuring that programmes supporting women take into account their care responsibilities;
5. promoting flexible routes from work to retirement; and
6. taking into account the complexity of transition from work to employment.

Nearly a decade later, employers still have a great deal to catch up on. Think about your organisation and the extent to which its practices support these six areas. If you have any concerns, you may need to consult your human resources department. You may have to play a role in bringing these issues to their attention. With luck, the department will be receptive to this information and will appreciate your interest and knowledge. One contribution you will be making is helping others in similar positions. This may be particularly important if your company suffers from that insidious prejudice: ageism.

Ageist Attitudes
Ageist attitudes towards older workers are bad for business, as the 'Managing Age' guide by the Trades Union Congress (TUC) and

the Chartered Institute of Personnel and Development (CIPD) clearly states:

> Age discrimination is bad for business because it causes an unnecessary waste of talent, skills, knowledge and experience as well as undermining social cohesion and personal achievement.

Yet, age discrimination is deeply embedded in the practices of many businesses, as well as in their organisational culture and policies. A 2010 Equality and Human Rights Commission report emphasised that 'many older people are keen to carry on working or to embark on new careers, but they often face obstacles caused by stereotyping, inflexibility or simple lack of imagination about how work could be organised differently', with many managers apparently resisting change.

Perceptions of older workers' abilities are often based on stereotypical images – that older workers are too cautious; slow in their work; or have decreased cognitive function. Some people believe that older workers find it hard to learn new skills, are more prone to ill health, have lower productivity, or even that they are simply marking time before retiring. It is essential that these misconceptions are challenged wherever possible. As Ken Robinson, an adviser on education, creativity and economics, puts it in his book on accessing creativity, *Out of Our Minds*:

> Declining birth rates mean that employers are going to have to become more creative if they want to access the knowledge workers need. And that means abandoning the lazy prejudice of age discrimination.

Employers share the dominant attitudes of our culture that link physical decline with 60th birthdays. These assumptions by employers need challenging as much as they do in the general population. 'There is little evidence that chronological age is a strong determinant of health, cognitive or physical abilities, sickness absence, work-related injuries or productivity,' concluded the Health and Safety Executive in a review of research into age and employment. It went on to suggest that performance is unlikely to decrease even with reduced capability, 'because most jobs do not require employees to work at full capacity'. The common misconception that older workers are less capable persists and is the basis of many ageist assumptions.

Ageist attitudes have distressing outcomes. Although it is unlawful to apply age criteria when recruiting, either on job advertisements or in selection processes, some employers are nonetheless reluctant to recruit older workers. It can be hard to prove that your job application has been turned down solely for reasons of age discrimination, but certainly the statistics bear up the suspicion that workers in the 50-plus age group experience greater difficulties when they are out of work and seeking employment. Figures from the Department for Work & Pensions reveal that older workers are more likely to be long-term unemployed: 44 per cent of the over-50s have been unemployed longer than a year compared with 30 per cent of people under 50, and this is despite them being more likely to work part-time.

Even those already in employment can face age discrimination. Some employers are reluctant to adapt to older workers' needs and aspirations, for example by failing to provide training or adapt working environments. This is despite the fact that many workers in the 50-plus age group want promotion, and 62 per cent describe themselves as being as fit as ever. Many who have chosen to work for longer are happy and enjoying what they do. It seems that it is the managers of older workers who most need the retraining.

The good news is that some ageist behaviours are changing and negative attitudes are becoming less publicly acceptable, as well as being illegal, in the workplace.

Indeed, one or two firms have made a virtue of employing older people, such as the hardware store B&Q, where their wisdom and experience, as well as their sympathetic attitude to less confident craftspeople, make them more approachable to customers.

The store's website claims that diversity in their employment policy makes sound business sense, as well as being the right thing to do.

Asda has also pioneered a deliberate policy of employing older workers. The Broadstairs store in Kent 'deliberately recruited 25 per cent of [older] staff to break the nervousness of management around absence, labour turnover and capability of older workers', said Caroline Massingham, people director for the chain, in a *Guardian* report in November 2011. Among the advantages she lists are the positive effects upon the working environment, the mentoring of younger employees and increased stability in the workforce.

The UK could also learn from practice in Finland, where the Finnish National Programme for Ageing Workers requires government and other organisations to develop initiatives to help businesses with flexible retirement and to combat ageist attitudes. The programme provides incentives such as higher pensions for those who continue to work. Policy development in the UK is more piece-meal and relies heavily on the goodwill of employers. In difficult times employers react to the short-term, to policy pressures and to the habit of using older workers as a buffer within their workforce. 'A substantial change in attitude towards how older workers are viewed and how the issue of retirement is approached' is required according to the TUC and the CIPD guidance.

Until that time comes, if you have been on the receiving end of age discrimination in your workplace it's always worth challenging it. That's where a support group or union can be very helpful in giving you the confidence to speak up, rather than leave work under a cloud.

Flexible Working Arrangements

Age discrimination is not the only factor holding back older workers. It seems that employers are also dragging their feet to accommodate older workers' need for more flexibility in working arrangements. These include hours, routes out of work and preventative approaches to health issues. Employers who take account of these are likely to get more from their workforce. The government will extend the right to request flexible working arrangements to all employees in 2014 – currently limited to carers.

'Many employers are currently missing a trick and are losing key talent from their organisations by failing to offer flexibility in the workplace,' states the CIPD. In evidence to the House of Lords, the CIPD claimed that 76 per cent of older workers reported that their employers had made no reasonable adjustments to requests to help them continue in work.

Would some flexibility in your working arrangements help you? Have a word with your boss. It's worth asking. Something you suggest might help the organisation as well.

Bridging Jobs

A bridging job is a post specifically designed for older workers who still have much to offer, but not necessarily by continuing in the same post. The new role forms a bridge into retirement. It may have modified physical demands, or include mentoring of less experienced workers.

BT, with 32 per cent of its workforce over 50, has developed flexible working practices. The head of BT's diversity practice refers to accommodating the needs of the 'grandparenting' community among the older workers. These practices help delay retirement and include:

- wind down (part-time or job-share posts);
- step down (reduced responsibilities);
- time out (sabbatical);
- helping hand (charity or community work); and
- ease down (reducing hours in the 12 months prior to retirement).

A few older workers find that their capacities have declined in ways that affect their work. According to the Equality Act 2010, employers have a duty to make 'reasonable adjustments' to help workers of all ages with disability to remain in work. For some, it may be appropriate to reduce the burdens or responsibilities, sometimes called downshifting. Others may require a change in work arrangements. For example, for those with cardiovascular and respiratory decline, modifications might include: changes in work design or use of equipment for lifting; restrictions on the amount of lifting and other heavy physical tasks; or an increased number of breaks. An example would be a nurse who is no longer able to lift patients, but who still has many skills that are needed in the NHS. Other modifications are appropriate for workers who have declining sensory functions, such as hearing, musculoskeletal function, and psychological conditions such as depression.

Do you want to: wind down, step down, have time out, give a helping hand or ease down? Let your voice be heard.

Re-Employment

Employers may negotiate a more flexible role with their older workers, perhaps even after retiring. Examples include continuing to work as a researcher or supervising students at a university. A fee-paid arrangement, more like a consultancy, can provide both sides with advantages: the employer benefits from the experiences and skills of their former employee, and the employee can work flexibly, perhaps with reduced hours and reduced stress.

Some companies are already seeking to fill a skills gap with former employees. One retired engineer, asking for advice in the *Guardian*'s Work section in 2012, described his own rather fortunate situation, torn between wanting to go back to work and carrying on to enjoy his retirement: 'I am a retired professional engineer, living very comfortably on my pension and voluntary redundancy payment accumulated after 42 years with one company. This former company, now very short of engineers, is unable to find younger engineers and is looking to take on retirees on what are very lucrative short-term contracts. I am struggling to decide whether to become re-employed.' The helpful response was along the lines of: you are not making an irrevocable decision so go for it, for as long as it suits you.

To make these arrangements work, employers need to pay attention to the resource needs of such workers: desk space, access to computers, administrative support and the ability to be linked into communications about workplace developments. Clearly negotiated roles, perhaps a job description, can help this arrangement. This information needs to be available to all staff. Retirees working in the organisation also need development and supervision, especially if they are involved in mentoring or coaching, or are working with young people. In other words, retirees need to be given the same respect as other workers. We are aware that flexible arrangements are in the main available only to more skilled workers, who are already well placed in the job market. The public sector organisations are significantly more likely to offer flexible working than the private sector. For some workers flexibility can mean insecurity of employment.

However, if you fancy a more flexible role – go for it!

Three Kinds of Arrangements for Flexible Hours

The most obvious flexibility in hours is through part-time work. This may suit you. A recruitment campaign for bus drivers in Brisbane, Australia, specifically targeted retired workers, with a campaign that featured combining the job with activities such as golf and spending time with grandchildren. Oh no, not golf and grandchildren again! Some of you may want to substitute these with activities such as ballroom dancing and a trip to the pub.

The second kind is the gradual reduction in hours towards retirement, in one or more stages. In most countries, workers phase into retirement through reduction in hours. This is rare in the UK but becoming more common. A smooth transition from employment to retirement can benefit both employer and employee.

The third kind of flexibility is to accommodate unpredictable demands placed upon workers in their role as a carer. An older worker might welcome flexibility to choose and vary their hours, flexi-time. Carers are entitled to request flexible work arrangements.

Would one of these arrangements suit you? Think about the advantages and disadvantages of each of these arrangements before asking for a change in your work situation.

Flexible Location

Being flexible about where work can be done – the home, a cafe or elsewhere, as it suits you – is only appropriate for some kinds of work, such as producing designs or text that can be electronically communicated. But this kind of flexibility, where it is possible, can benefit you if you also have caring responsibilities or have a form of disability, or want to fit in work alongside other activities. Some businesses have closed their offices and expect employees to work at home, as Nick – a building inspector – found out. He has built an office in his garden. He likes the extra time not journeying to work that every day affords.

Job-Shares

Job-shares have long been popular with women with care responsibilities. They offer the possibility of doing a high-quality job, without being full-time. For older workers and their employers, another attraction of job-sharing is the opportunity to work alongside a younger worker and to guide and teach them, a kind of mentoring or coaching role.

The reports we consulted point to the need for much more to be done to offer flexible opportunities such as these. Responsibility lies with the employee as well as the employer for changes to accommodate older workers, and employers in the UK lead the field in these respects. This is both good news and worrying information for those of us who work in the UK. It clearly still needs to improve.

Whether you are female or male, a job-share may suit you. The attraction is that you can still work at the same level but have more time to pursue activities outside work. This is a good way of trying out possibilities for when you eventually retire.

Retraining and Training Opportunities

Being treated as if you have already gone, or are on the point of departure, is a very dispiriting experience. A frequent false assumption by employers is that older workers do not want or need further training or professional development. Again, it's good business to achieve the best quality workforce and be up-to-the-minute in training. Some employers assume that investment in younger employees is more efficient, but the contrary is true. 'In fact, training an older worker will bring returns to the employer, while training a younger worker will benefit one's competitors,' researchers in Oxford have claimed in a survey of global retirement practices and attitudes to older workers. The public sector is a better employer in this respect, providing much more training to older workers than the private sector does.

Many older workers are enthusiastic about taking on new challenges. One example is the unpredicted uptake of apprenticeships by older workers, the so-called 'silver apprentices'. In November 2011 it was revealed that there has been an increase in apprenticeships for younger people (18–24 year olds) of around 20 per cent, but for the over-60s the growth has been nearly 900 per cent. Yes, 900 per cent. Putting percentages into figures reveals that, out of the grand total of 163,000 apprenticeships, 400 over-60s signed up in 2009–10, and 3,910 in the next year. The coverage might have given the impression that apprenticeships were being gobbled up by the over-60s. In fact, they are taking up 2.4 per cent of the opportunities, about one in every 50. The picture is of resourceful older workers, demonstrating a willingness to retrain or even receive training for the first time.

Graham Egginton is one such silver apprentice, starting his apprenticeship just before his 57th birthday. He had been unemployed for 14 months following the liquidation of the machinery business where he had previously worked. He now works as a technical service engineer with Centrica, the energy company, in Wolverhampton. 'Initially it was a case of "I need a job". But I've ended up quite enjoying it. I want to go on to 65 at least,' Graham told the researchers at the Equality and Human Rights Commission.

Appraisal and performance management systems are as beneficial for employers with older workers as for those with a younger workforce. Not only do they encourage high-performance working practices, but they also allow employers to develop improvement strategies, build skills and improve organisational capacity.

Why not check out the opportunities for apprenticeships if you are interested in this idea, and ask your manager for an appraisal meeting if you haven't had one for some time?

Employers Supporting the Decision to Leave – How (and How Not) to Do It

A good employer is as careful about investing in the well-being of employees approaching the end of their career as it is about the induction of new staff. Such employers demonstrate a clear commitment to the needs of their workforce. The decision about the date of retirement, the ability to take time over this decision, the need for knowledge about pensions and life after work – all these can be assisted by the employer.

Good practice includes:

- a well-publicised retirement policy;
- the provision of information, especially about pensions;
- the provision of support for making decisions, through seminars and workshops, coaching and mentoring; and
- ensuring a good farewell.

Employers need to consider how to prepare and help their employees make decisions that suit their individual needs. Having a well-publicised retirement policy is a good start, as it requires all staff members to adopt good practice and a positive approach to retirement. An effective retirement policy covers its purpose, the actions and practices that are expected of managers and retirees, and the entitlement of employees to the rituals of leaving. As workers approach retirement, managers need to be aware of the possibilities for flexibility in employment and the value of phased retirement.

See if you can locate your organisation's retirement policy. If there isn't one, ask for a meeting with your manager to discuss your options. It would be useful to prepare for this meeting beforehand, listing all the things you want to find out. It might also be a good idea to go to the meeting with a friend or colleague so that they can take notes and discuss the outcomes of the meeting with you afterwards.

A poor understanding of pension entitlements is unfortunately very common among employees. A third of employees 'do not even have a rough idea of what their pensions may pay out', calculated the National Association of Pension Funds. Research has shown that lack of knowledge may be a barrier to workers continuing in employment, as the following responses show:

- 40 per cent of people would consider delaying their retirement if they could defer their state pension in return for higher payments;
- 59 per cent are unaware that this option already exists;
- 42 per cent would consider delaying their retirement if they could combine income from their occupational pension and their current job; and
- 60 per cent are unaware that this option is already available to many employees.

Employer-run briefing sessions on pensions and pension choices can help people plan more efficiently the financial aspects of retirement. Access to, or information about, sources of professional financial advice is also very valuable. Ask your employer if such briefing sessions exist in your organisation and see if your human resources department has any information to pass on.

Workshops or seminars that encourage participants to consider the transitions of retirement can also help prepare for other aspects of life. These can be provided in-house or places can be bought on courses by dedicated providers. Sharing ideas and plans can help counter some stereotyped or downbeat attitudes towards retirement. Providing different perspectives can be life changing for people who have been too busy to consider all the possibilities. One participant in a recent workshop, for example, reported that she had been talking to some frustrated retired friends, who told her that their lives were very boring. As a result she was afraid that boredom in retirement was her destiny. Another participant immediately reported the case of his friend who had taken the opportunity of retiring from her work as a librarian to retrain as a curate and was now enjoying her new, busy occupation. These anecdotal experiences reinforce the great differences in perception about retirement, and it is easy to see how they could affect one's own feelings on the subject.

Workshops we have run have explored the topics covered in the second half of this book. Some of our workshop participants, having enjoyed the interactive and mutual benefits of the sessions, have gone on to create their own support groups. These are not difficult to set up. Ask colleagues if they would be interested and give it a go. You may be surprised by the value of such an experience.

Participation in a workshop programme contributes to reduced levels of anxiety, stress and depression, greater satisfaction, more post-retirement social activity and increased well-being in retirement, according to reviews. Seminars and other programmes that help people prepare for retirement have risen substantially in the last decade. We can confirm from the experiences of those in our retiring group, of participants in our retiring workshops and of individuals we have coached that thinking ahead promotes satisfaction in retirement.

If you think that joining a workshop, course or support group would benefit you, then you will find helpful the ideas in chapter 6. That chapter also looks at coaching and other forms of support.

Coaching can also provide a framework for the preparation and planning of retirement. In a coaching session you will be given the opportunity to explore any ambivalence you might experience as you approach retirement. You can envision a preferred future and begin the necessary steps to achieve it. And you can be led to consider the experiences of others, to illuminate your own transitions.

A good ending requires organisational awareness. We received an example recently from an employee retiring from the railways. He was given two weeks to travel without a specific brief, except to visit all the sites where he had worked and to say goodbye to his colleagues. This practice demonstrates a respect for the achievements of the person leaving, their work relationships and a value of good endings.

But a common experience for older workers in their final months is to be ignored or marginalised and not be included in succession planning. We received the following account from Raymond Carter, after he had read an article we wrote about good practice. He told us that he was summoned to discuss his request to take early retirement. He had a meeting that lasted two minutes with his line manager. 'I was told to ensure that my office was completely cleared in a month. There were no expressions of sorrow or gratitude or even curiosity about my future plans and no acknowledgement of what I had accomplished for the institution. I now have mixed feelings about my impending retirement. I am bitter about the lack of acknowledgement for what I have achieved for the university.' The way in which an employer handles – or mishandles – a retiree's departure can contribute greatly to the quality of that person's transitions out of work.

One of the few key events in your transition is likely to be your retirement party. For many it is a ritual that provides an opportunity for goodbyes, thank-yous, tributes and the acknowledgement of all that an individual has contributed to the organisation and their field throughout their career. Not everyone will want such an event, but every organisation should offer to plan this with the retiree and contribute to its success. This needs to be done wholeheartedly. Think about whether you want a party or whether another form of leaving event might be more acceptable.

Post-Retirement Connections: Alumni, Volunteering, Social and Other Events

It doesn't have to end there. After the speeches at your retirement party have been made, your workload and workspace allocated to a successor, you may wish to continue your connection to the organisation. Universities have long recognised this, and benefited from a system of *alumni*, which is a formal association with the university. For some alumni there are responsibilities to make a contribution, such as mentoring colleagues or advising on research projects. Other alumni may wish to continue the intellectual connection with former colleagues, by assisting with projects for example.

You may want to continue your social connections, perhaps by retaining your work email address, which allows you to access former colleagues and be involved in some of the internal communications. You may wish to be invited to social events such as Christmas celebrations and formal occasions.

You may also wish to volunteer on behalf of the organisation, both in-house and out. Examples include mentoring colleagues in-house as alumni members, volunteering out-of-house, and offering your professional skills on a pro bono basis.

Closing Thoughts

While the balance has shifted towards individual decisions, especially about the timing of retirement, employers carry a responsibility for their older workers. Employers offering flexible employment in later years and helping employees prepare for retirement, as well as a good send-off, will support people to make good transitions, and to continue to make valuable contributions beyond their retirement dates. This attitude and practice make for a better workplace for all employees.

You can be active in encouraging your employer to provide support for your decisions about when and how to leave. There's lots you can consider – do the research, get information and advice, demand your rights, get politically active, talk to your union rep, get your voice heard, form a support group. It will be fun and satisfying as well as productive.

Chapter 4
Learning *through* Retirement

Learning is the best strategy humans have to deal with change. It is therefore extraordinary that so little attention is paid to informal and unstructured learning in retiring. So much learning takes place every day that we take it for granted. You already have a great deal of experience in informal and unstructured learning – from previous transitions and changes in your life, from self-reflections and making plans – so you have insights and wisdom to draw on now.

You probably don't think too much about your learning, but here are three good reasons why you should:

- Learning can support your transitions into retirement, help you navigate the changes along the way and make better decisions.
- Learning occurs through your everyday living, especially in social situations.
- Learning happens all through your retirement years, in response to the changes you experience, as a continuation of a lifelong process.

We've thought a lot about learning and are passionate about it. It's been the focus of our professional work for decades. This chapter draws on our knowledge to help you secure a successful retirement through learning.

Making Sense of Learning

A good place to start being explicit about your learning is to notice the stage of retiring you're in – are you just looking, making preparations, in the process of retiring, a novice making adjustments to your new life, or a veteran enjoying your new status? And to go over what you have already learned, compare your thoughts with the following list. Participants in a retiring workshop were surprised by how much they had learned about:

- practical issues (knowledge and information about what forms to fill out);
- previous experiences of major change (reactions and strategies that helped them adapt);
- their feelings (excitement about new opportunities, ambivalence, and anxiety about finances);
- living arrangements (will their accommodation still be appropriate?);
- the expectations of others (about new roles, changing friendships);
- using skills and knowledge in a new context (mentoring and coaching);
- surprises (how they were valued by their colleagues);
- dissonant feelings (wanting to be retired but afraid of losing opportunities to be involved in something important);
- challenges to their identity ('Who will I be when I no longer work?');
- their sense of self (where to find purpose in life); and
- the next changes to make ('Where do I want to be in a year's time, in five years' time?').

You will have noticed that some aspects of learning are quite straightforward, like finding the right forms. But these workshop participants were also considering more abstract concepts, such as the development of understanding, thinking in a new way and changing as a person. These conceptions of learning are hierarchical, meaning that more complex processes are required for more sophisticated changes and transitions.

One retirement workshop attendee, Janet, gave an example that demonstrates this complexity. She was planning to retire from her work as a probation officer within the next 18 months. A major evaluation of the service was due in that time. She dreaded this for two reasons. First, she felt it would not be the culmination of her career that she had hoped for and, second, the process of evaluation would not help the organisation. Things had changed a lot for her. Indeed she had come to see that she wanted to leave the organisation because her work no longer fulfilled her values. The prospect of further change was intimidating.

From discussions in the retiring workshops she came to see that the death of her husband and a second marriage had provided her with considerable experience of dealing with change, including many unwanted changes. She also reaffirmed to herself that it was important to do work that she believed in, especially as she did not need the money. She did, however, choose to steer her department through the external evaluation, out of a sense of loyalty to her colleagues and to the service she had once valued. Janet came to understand her own values and priorities, her own skills, and how to plan a way through this turbulent period.

To live is to learn – it's as simple as that. Learning is a human activity. It's what people do, as Janet's reflections demonstrate. And we do it throughout our lives, especially at times of transitions and change. We use the word 'change' to refer to alterations in situations: for example, moving house, a revision to a pension plan, leaving full-time employment. 'Transition', on the other hand, is more internal, relating to how you think, act and respond to new situations, and most importantly how you see yourself.

All change can provide rich opportunities for learning, for example in gaining and adjusting to new identities, in developing new skills, knowledge and wisdom, in thinking about the course of your life and in challenging assumptions about what you should and shouldn't do. Learning can help you recover from bad experiences and create the life you want. And most important of all it prevents you from feeling helpless in the face of challenges and difficulties.

It's crucial to remember that people never stop learning. We seek order in our lives, make connections, find solutions and handle conflicting views – just as Janet has done. We also seek new perspectives and resolve disorienting dilemmas, seek meaning, continue to understand ourselves and our actions, and anticipate events. We can also plan, and can often control events rather than be ruled by them. This is especially useful in times of change and ambiguity.

This sort of learning is learned but can't be taught. It happens informally when we adjust to new circumstances and interruptions in our lives. Retiring can be seen as a turning point – a productive time for learning when changes in our circumstances force us to think differently and make sense of our lives and what we are going to do. We need to notice the learning as it happens in order to make sense of it.

You have experienced many turning points or interruptions in your life, such as leaving home, committing yourself to another adult, having children. Retiring is another such turning point. It brings both an opportunity for applying what you have learned previously and a chance for creating a new understanding in order to make the best of retirement's changes and transitions.

Learning in Retirement

Every aspect of your life changes in retirement. The changes can be large or small, sudden or gradual. You need to make sense of them, and to some extent be prepared for them. Your financial situation is likely to change, as are the demands upon your time. You will also undergo transitions – for example, your sense of who you are. The transitions involved in retirement are substantial and provide opportunities for self-reflection and finding ways to sustain a long-held identity in new circumstances.

Retiring is not a single event but a series of transitions taking place over a number of years. You start as a novice and graduate to veteran status. Novice retirees are still adjusting to the changes in their arrangements of daily activities, relationships, finances and their sense of themselves. Veterans are more experienced, more adjusted to these changes, have even been able to change things in order to meet their needs, perhaps through negotiating with friends and family. Seeing retiring as a series of events provides opportunities for learning at every stage.

You could also see retirement as crossing a boundary, moving from a life largely shaped by paid work to a life with other determinants, such as caring for others, travel, voluntary work, involvement in your other interests. You learn new knowledge, skills and self-awareness, both as you cross the boundary and when you find yourself on the other side of it. This image of a crossing appears to contradict the idea of retirement as a series of changes, but it makes sense if you think of the boundary not as a brief moment in time, but rather as a period of months, even years.

In the outdated version of retirement the crossing was often brief, abrupt and marked by the retirement party and a gift (traditionally an oddly symbolic gold watch). Many experienced it as a violent moment of sudden changes. Today more gentle transitions are possible. Caroline describes herself as 'retired but still working', and is still within the boundary zone. In contrast, Josephine who retired from teaching six years ago, sees herself as beyond the boundary, a veteran. Recently she said that she was 'fully transitioned', meaning she has adapted to her changed life and no longer looks back to her working life as a reference point or feels connected to the organisation for which she worked. Self-reflection, as Caroline and Josephine show, helps make sense of changes and any disorienting dilemmas.

You can boost your own complex learning by reflecting on the events and changes you are facing: recognising the emotional ambiguities you may be feeling, seeing your experiences in a new way, developing new skills and understanding your own habits. They all result in understanding the world in new ways and having a different outlook, even becoming a different person.

The first thing to do in handling a transition is to recognise that you have to let something go. It may involve seeing yourself in a new light and understanding the various phases you need to go through. You may need to develop new skills for negotiating the transition, and it is useful to understand the way you have coped with endings in the past. Talk with others about your transitions as this may be helpful.

Have a look at the following list. It contains 10 ways of maximising your chances of finding meaning in the change from work to retiring. It has been developed from *Transitions: Making Sense of Life's Changes* by the American author William Bridges.

1. **Take your time** – There are many stages from work to retirement and you don't need to rush through them. Allow yourself to catch up with the different changes. Take a break from the process of retiring sometimes by engaging with unrelated activities.

2. **Arrange temporary structures** – Reduce your hours to experience a shorter working week. Rent accommodation in the area where you plan to live. Join a group of people who are also retiring to share your thoughts.

3. **Don't act for the sake of action** – Other people will be experiencing things differently and you don't have to do things their way. Take steps when you are ready.

4. **Recognise why you are feeling uncomfortable** – Discomfort or distress are not necessarily a sign of anything going wrong, but of change. Expect ambivalence, anxiety, highs and lows.

5. **Take care of yourself in little ways** – Don't abandon your routines and comforting activities all at once. Give yourself treats or rewards.

6. **Explore the far side of change** – If you have been forced into retirement for whatever reason, look at the opportunities it offers. If you have chosen the circumstances of your retirement, explore the less desirable consequences as well.

7. **Get someone to talk to** – Tell the story of your retirement to others as well as yourself – it can be transforming. Join a group. Find a coach.

8. **Find out what's waiting in the wings** – Consider what might be waiting to happen in your life when you give up work and have more time – a novel, a reunion, a cruise, learning to play the trombone. Take a few risks, have fun.

9. **Use every transition as the impetus to a new kind of learning** – Be conscious of how you approach the changes and transitions, and draw on your previous experiences, such as moving house or taking up a new job.

10. **Recognise that a transition has a characteristic shape** – Notice that change involves beginnings, transitional times and endings, and draw on your experiences for strategies to deal with these, such as seeking help from others or taking smaller steps.

You might want to consider which aspects in this list are the most important to you and identify the things that you want to do straight away. Talk about your plans with others.

Learning to Be – Finding a New Identity in Retirement

As you move through the stages of retirement, aspects of your identity may be unclear. 'How will I think of myself?' and 'How will others think of me?' are two important questions – if I am no longer a head teacher, an entrepreneur, a journalist, a consultant, then who am I? Am I anybody? What purposes do I have in my life? We have found that these themes emerge frequently in retiring groups, workshops, coaching and in conversations. How will I know my worth, and how will others know my worth if I have no job?

'Learning to be' is a simple idea based on the concept of the complete person's fulfilment. It is described in an important UNESCO report called 'Learning: The Treasure Within' by Jacques Delors. The aim is to help you create the life you want and it is particularly appropriate in contexts of change, complexity and uncertainty. If we look at this idea in terms of the transition from novice retiree to veteran, we can see that three areas are particularly important.

Learning to Leave Aspects of Your Life Behind

In order to find fulfilment, retirees must learn to leave aspects of their lives behind as they cross the boundary from work to retiring. They must learn not to work any more. One of the hardest things to leave behind is the definition of yourself provided by a job or profession. While employed, a job is an easy index for what the world needs to know about you. Richard Ford, an American novelist, suggests that your work gives an idea to others of what you are worth, and many would argue that it says something about your character, values, moral responsibility and self-awareness. Of course a job does not define an individual any more than any other label, and it can in fact easily mask a person's character. A person's identity is not the same as their job or profession, although they may be very closely bound together. But in the world's eyes the two are often seen as inextricably linked.

Focusing on losing a work identity is part of the outdated view of retiring. It focuses on what you no longer are, rather than on the aspects of your life that will continue and those that you will develop. You could say there are three parts to the task – one: identifying what is to be left behind; but more importantly two: identifying what you want to retain; and three: who you want to be.

Among the things you will leave behind are salary, structure to your day, a work community. Some of these things will be important and you may have to learn how to let go or replace them. And as you become involved in new activities, you will find new ways of thinking about your role in your communities and in the world. To a large extent this 'learning to be' will happen informally, in everyday life and in social situations.

Finding New Identities

The processes of 'learning to be', of developing a new identity, can be assisted by telling your story and sharing your experiences with others. These activities can help you develop and rehearse new identities.

Alex Moore, a professor in education, surprised himself when he wrote about his transition into retirement in *Retiring Lives*. Sorting his thoughts into words as he wrote helped him make sense of his feelings:

> It has proved a curiously therapeutic exercise – like all good therapy helping me through and beyond a difficult transition in much quicker time than I could reasonably have hoped had I been left to my own devices. The pressure that I was putting on myself (the pressure to 'achieve', or perhaps the pressure of self-accusation at *not having achieved*) has gone: it has ebbed away as I have thought about it and written about it, until now it appears a vestige.

Finding and accepting new identities are major tasks of 'learning to be' in retirement. This idea may appear daunting, as a retiree must leave behind the familiar and develop a new sense of self. This new sense is not applied in a narrow way, like becoming a gardener or a painter, but in a much broader way, such as discovering what you are capable of or want to be, and finding the means to achieve fulfilment. For people approaching retirement and in the novice zone, this means working towards the desired future without a focus on employment.

Eileen remembers how retirement challenged her own sense of self, but she found that talking to friends about her situation and practising her new identity in public helped her. She needed to wrestle with different images and experiment with the different narratives of a retiring person before she felt comfortable with her new self-image. Being part of an active network of friends in the same situation enabled her to practise these new behaviours without judgment or criticism, and writing reflectively about her feelings further helped to make the process of learning more explicit. She had to work on embracing a new way of being – both with herself and with other people.

A person's identity is actively constructed as they continually integrate new events into their account of their lives, suggests Anthony Giddens, a prominent sociologist. And it can be difficult if this new identity requires significant adjustment to the story that they told themselves previously. If you had been a senior manager, for example, and told yourself that you were highly influential in your place of work, that people relied on you to make decisions and resolve difficult tensions, then leaving that role and its related identity for quite a different life may be very difficult to come to terms with.

The involvement of others in the redefinition of your identity is also significant, so your social setting is important in its formation. How your friends, family, former colleagues, neighbours and community come to see you will influence how you see yourself.

It can be hard to develop a new sense of yourself in the face of the social practices and prejudices of other people. For example, introductions to participants in TV game shows often go like this: 'What do you do, Brenda?' 'I'm retired.' 'What did you do before you retired?'… It's as if a retired person does nothing and their identity is tied up with what they no longer do. You may hate the label 'retired' – many do – as it's often associated with inactivity and dependence, and it is frequently a very inaccurate description. Or you may hate being labelled by what you did before. Caroline met Valerie during the coffee break of a daytime adult education class. She talked about her active life attending classes. She was in her third year of learning Arabic and being a member of a political reading group. She had retired 20 years earlier. 'Thank you for not asking me what I did before I retired,' she said. 'I hated that job and I do not want to be defined by it now.'

To help develop your new identity in retirement, you can continue to use an established identity for a while in order to feel secure and comfortable. Many retirees do this. We know many people who work as consultants and take on short-term contracts for the type of work they did before. Teachers often take on roles as school governors.

Others start creating a different existence and a different identity. In a conversation with us, Desmond said that while he was getting his bearings and waiting for satisfactory responses from others, he took gradual steps to establish his new self. He explained how he handed over his plumbing business to his son when he retired and took up painting. He built a studio in his garden and 'started to dabble'. Four years on, he was persuaded by his son to mount an exhibition of his paintings in his local cafe. Many people, including his ex-clients, bought his artworks. He stopped saying he dabbled and called himself an artist.

Here is the heart of 'learning to be' – creating the life you want and feeling contented. The answers to the question 'Who will I be in retirement?' gradually emerge, of course. New identities are embraced. You learn to leave behind the limits of your former labels, whether these were self-imposed or put upon you by others. You learn not just to give up work, but also to embrace what is on the other side of the boundary, and learn to truly be.

Four suggestions, adapted from William Bridges, can support you with 'learning to be':

- **Stop getting ready and act** – What is the first thing you will do as a retired person? Decide and then do it! Visit your grandchildren, book a cruise, enrol on a course ...

- **Begin to identify yourself with the result of the change** – Play with some descriptions: 'I am an artist', 'I care for my mother', 'I'm writing my first novel'.
- **Take things step-by-step** – Try out new roles. Resist the idea that there is a more exciting and meaningful route.
- **Set out to understand the process of learning, do not focus only on the ultimate goal** – Reflect on the effects of your actions, your new knowledge, the new dimension of yourself.

Here is another account of a new identity emerging. Sheila woke one morning not knowing who she was any more after 38 years of working as a nurse in a busy city hospital. She was divorced and her husband had remarried. Her two children both lived abroad and most of her friends were still working. She felt lonely and her only comfort was in attending church and talking with other parishioners. This was not how she anticipated her life would be. She talked with her doctor who prescribed her anti-depressants, but she didn't want to take them. A local discussion group was helpful and she realised a way of overcoming unwanted thoughts and feelings, and was able to develop a more positive outlook. With the support of the group, she visited her cousins in Ireland whom she had not seen for many years. She started to research her family tree. She found it fascinating to talk with relatives about their memories of their grandparents, and it helped her to learn about herself by exploring her roots.

Sheila's account of learning through her retirement involved learning about her own feelings, both of her unhappiness at her lone-liness and her dissatisfaction with the prescription of anti-depressants as a possible solution. Learning from new relationships, especially within her discussion group and then her relatives, allowed her to explore her new experiences over time.

Being open-minded is one of the key attributes of *learning to be*. Both Sheila and Desmond set out to explore a new way of being, found a sense of purpose in their lives and a new identity – Sheila as the family historian and Desmond as an artist. But it can take some time. Neither Sheila nor Desmond thought too much about their retirement in advance. Luckily, in time they became aware of ways of being that fulfilled them. You may want to construct your new identity in a planned way by taking more control over what is happening to you.

Reconsidering Your Values in Retirement

In finding contentment in retirement it's important to reconsider the values and attitudes you live by. This will affirm what you do, how you find purpose in retirement, how you relate to other people and how you select the activities you engage in. Values are a major influence on our prospects for achieving a contented retiring life and in learning to be.

We may not think about our values very much. But feelings of discomfort are a good signal that we need to take notice and align our actions with our values. This is exactly what happened to Janet, the probation officer we introduced earlier. She wanted to leave her workplace because it conflicted with her values, and she left work to find new activities that matched her values. On the other hand, we may feel uneasy or lost when we leave behind aspects of our working lives that we found fulfilling. We are faced with finding other activities to replace them, and our long-term principles are used to judge the worth of our ideas or actions. They provide the criteria by which we decide whether something is good or right for us, and whether we want to be involved.

In retiring we will feel satisfied if our lives reflect our values. Some of our values are based on moral or religious beliefs, some are social or cultural, and others aesthetic and creative. It is no surprise that many retirees continue to do the sort of things that they have been interested in and committed to all their lives. Your choice of work may well have been based on your values and views of moral responsibility, as is the case with Sir Brendan Barber. Barber, who retired recently after a 10-year period as general secretary at the TUC, now has a part-time post as chair of the Advisory, Conciliation and

Arbitration Service. Many people continue with pursuing political interests and participating in formal education. Many retirees work as volunteers for Voluntary Service Overseas, act as trustees, mentors and coaches or as magistrates. These retirees want to continue to serve others and pass on their wisdom. Others see their communities as a place where they can serve and support others. Family relationships are paramount for many, and some are fulfilled through being good neighbours and citizens. Receiving MBEs in the 2013 New Year's Honours List came as a complete surprise to Mary and John Richardson from Exmouth, Devon. Their recognition of being good citizens was for their lifetime work as foster parents. Now, both aged 80, Mary and John are still fostering teenagers. Others find fulfilment elsewhere. We read again and again how spending time in learning, studying, writing, creative activities and being involved in the arts are particularly nourishing for retirees. Finding the sort of activities that reflect one's values may come easily to you, but it is worth reassessing if all the different dimensions of your life are being fulfilled.

Our workshops and research activities provide much evidence of retirees who find satisfaction in their day-to-day lives by using their time to help and support others. These acts of kindness help people who are lonely or unable to complete simple tasks in their homes. Many unsung heroes visit relatives and friends in hospitals and care homes, look after grandchildren and great-grandchildren, help partners and parents, run activities for older people in care centres – all celebrating the values of lifelong mutual support, dependence and interdependence.

Learning Together

Opportunities to learn in collaboration with others are especially rich, as personal meaning and understanding often arise through social interaction. Learning with others requires shared skills of communication, collaboration, interaction, interconnectivity, interdependence, sensitivity and empathy. These skills can themselves all be learned.

The power of learning with others – friends, interest communities, acquaintances, chance encounters and family members – should not be underestimated. However, your predecessors and friends' experiences of retirement may not always be a useful reference point. Your contemporaries, on the other hand, can be a resourceful group and can help with questions such as:

- What health checks might I need?
- How do I deal with family members who assume that I am at their beck and call?
- What are my feelings about retiring at the moment?
- How do I recognise if I am depressed?
- How can I best adapt my daily life in retirement?

Mavis told us that she regretted her financial preparations being undertaken in isolation. 'It took me a long time to work all this out for myself. It would have helped if I could have done this more collectively, gaining ideas from others,' she admitted when answering our questions about finances. You are likely to have to take the initiative in order to gain the kind of support Mavis refers to. You might find colleagues who are approaching retirement and invite them to join a group. Or perhaps you can find supportive people on a retiring course, through an online community or by advertising in your local library.

Closing Thoughts

Changes and transitions in retirement require you to give up familiar structures, which may generate anxiety or leave you feeling vulnerable. At the same time, you may also feel excited and energised, looking forward to new challenges. These changes and transitions provide opportunities for self-reflection and learning. The learning will be effective if you can draw on previous experiences, which will help you move forward with confidence.

There are many different aspects to retiring that call for you to reflect and adapt. Transitions may include adjusting to new roles, developing new identities, adapting to new relationships, readjusting to new lifestyles, being a part of new communities, finding purpose, restating your values, being healthy and coping with the ageing experience. Some changes will be welcome and managed without difficulty. Others you may fear and try to put off for as long as possible. Some may always be difficult. However, throughout all these changes and transitions there are opportunities for reflection and learning.

Although some transitions are huge, they may creep up on you slowly, such as how you view yourself as a retired person. You may seek support for this type of adjustment (e.g., through coaching), but often you can manage it on your own or with the support of family and friends in conversation or in retiring groups. Reflection *in* learning, as well as *on* learning, means thinking about the processes you are using, perhaps seeing the learning as 'slow', much like the Slow Food movement uses the word. Don't be surprised if this learning takes over a decade or more.

You should feel excited and reassured by the idea that you are the author of your own changing narrative, and should relish the prospect of creating new positive outlooks and identities in retirement. Enjoy the learning.

Chapter 5

Occupation 'Retired'

How to reply to the question, 'So what do you do?' What to write in that space: *Occupation*? The simple answer, the word 'retired', says more about what you don't do than what you do do.

So, what are people doing in retirement? 'Contributing to the social fabric,' according to the former Archbishop of Canterbury Rowan Williams when he opened a debate in the House of Lords on 'Older People: Their Place and Contribution in Society' on 14 December 2012. And also contributing to the 'economic fabric', he said, quoting figures from Age UK: £50 billion for caring and family maintenance. He was challenging a common view: 'We are becoming dangerously used to speaking and thinking of an ageing population as a problem, a burden on public purse and private resources.'

Perhaps retirement was once a quiet retreat, dominated by rest and poverty and waiting for the call from death. Social and economic redundancy was how sociologists described it. Today, people's lives are longer and more active. And by and large this generation is more affluent than its predecessors. Consequently, retirees are very busy – occupation: occupied.

Adjusting to different ways of organising and using time is one of the chief transitions of retiring. And as you travel through the zones, from novice to veteran retiree, it is likely to continue to change. 'So how do you spend your time?' retirees are asked.

Sometimes this is in the spirit of enquiry from those anticipating retirement. Frequently it is asked with the assumption that having more time is a problem for retirees. However, over and over again retirees are heard to wonder how they ever found time for work, as they are fully occupied in retirement.

Employment fills and shapes so much time that the opportunity to be active in the ways you want is one of the joys of retiring. Here we explore what it's like to be involved in the various activities listed below. We also scrutinise some of the unhelpful messages and beliefs that abound. To make life as rich and as fulfilling as possible you need to look ahead while approaching retirement, and you need to consider the ways in which you want to use new opportunities.

Activities in Retirement

The contributions of retired people – financial and social – are made through many activities, including:

- paid employment;
- volunteering;
- various interests;
- formal education;
- holidays; and
- doing nothing very much.

A few retirees do all of these and more, and a very few do none of them.

The most obvious change for a retired person is having more time available. The transition into unstructured time can be tricky when lives have been shaped by the rhythms and routines of work, and it can take a few years to adapt. Your ability to take advantage of the increased availability of time depends on your economic and family commitments, as well as your health. For the most fortunate, retiring provides an opportunity to embark on a period of fulfilment and purpose, lasting perhaps for a decade or two of good health and energy.

Some people want to tell retirees that they have a duty to stay active. 'There's no excuse to vegetate in retirement,' you will hear. This finger-wagging accompanies the claim that 'keeping your brain and body active is the key to a good retirement', as *Saga* magazine puts it. The market reinforces this pressure by promoting electronic devices, such as games and exercisers, all targeted at older people. Much public discussion about the lives of older people assumes that a fulfilling life is one that has purpose and meaning. We will consider the validity of this assumption later in this chapter.

Nevertheless, for many retirees purposeful activity is undertaken not only for its own sake, but also because it is experienced as a contribution to physical, social and mental well-being. Ending paid employment means losing useful structures and social connectivity. 'Needing a reason to get out of bed' is the phrase frequently used by people for whom work had structured their time and focused their purposes. People who have been self-employed, familiar with organising their own time, are perhaps at an advantage here. And even if work hasn't been central to your life or if you think it is timely to move on, your day presents a different relationship to time and to activities within the day.

Paid Employment

There are lots of reasons to continue working in retirement, or to return to it. They might include the following: benefiting from the financial rewards, making a more gradual transition into retirement, continuing to make a contribution, maintaining social connections, having a reason to get out of bed in the morning, responding to a request from an employer, or wanting to continue being defined by employment.

Professional people may enjoy occasional work as consultants and as freelance workers. It is an advantage that the amount of work is usually within their control. If you are unsure about a decision to continue working, remember that it is not irrevocable. Situations can change, responses can change, and moving into retirement has no blueprint or road map. The message is to work as much or as little as suits you and your friends or family.

Volunteering

'Older people are already the bedrock of volunteering in this country,' claims Age UK, countering the prevailing view of the older population as a burden. Here's an impressive statistic: 58 per cent of people aged over 65 take part in voluntary work. The evidence is striking. 'Over half the population believe that [volunteering] is part of what they should aspire to in later life,' according to research for the Department for Work & Pensions. You are living in a society whose members aspire to improve its social fabric. Generally people are unaware of the scale of older people's contributions.

Informal volunteering describes caring activities (e.g., looking after grandchildren, older family members, checking on neighbours and doing someone else's shopping). Formal volunteering, which refers to activities within organisations, is the focus of this section.

There is so much more to volunteering than working in a charity shop. Mary, one of our interviewees, told us that when she retired from her work as a further education special needs teacher she tried volunteering in her local charity shop, but she gained so little satisfaction that she gave it up. And that was the end of her attempts to volunteer. Her story demonstrates the lack of information about what is available and how to access it.

Compare Mary's tentative steps with those of Dawn Ryder, a community paediatrician, whose adventurous spirit took her to Nepal and South Africa to care for impoverished children and children with HIV/Aids when she retired, according to a report in the *Independent* on the 'wellderly'. Or compare our friends Frances who trained as a volunteer for the Samaritans and Margery who became a citizens' adviser.

Why Volunteer?

Some people are lifelong volunteers. Some are serial volunteers, having volunteered from time to time as their other commitments or interests had permitted them – they may have volunteered before their children were born, then again once family and work demands had reduced. And a third group is triggered into volunteering by a major event, perhaps the death of someone they cared for or retirement. All three groups are influenced by their social and employment backgrounds and by how their families brought them up. For some, there is the influence of religious faith, and having knowledge of and commitment to their neighbourhood.

People are often motivated to make a contribution and do things for other people. They also gain themselves three main benefits. First, they meet new people and make friends. Second, they feel needed and, third, they gain confidence. Older volunteers also report wanting to structure their free time and continue to use skills from their working life, as well as respond to new opportunities that were not available to them while they were busy with a career.

Volunteers of all ages in the formal sector report a mixture of motives for volunteering and for choosing a particular activity:

Motive	Examples
To keep their brain active	The most frequently mentioned motivation by older volunteers and often referred to as 'a reason to get up in the morning'.
To occupy their time in meaningful ways	There can be a lot of free time in retirement, and for many people it is important that they use it doing something worthwhile.
To help others	Volunteering with any number of charities such as Age UK, Samaritans, Oxfam, Citizens Advice Bureau, Voluntary Service Overseas or prison visiting, and many, many more. Driving patients to hospital appointments, helping out in schools.

To give something back	Volunteering to help at a sports event, museum or art gallery.
To contribute to their local community	Becoming parish councillors, school governors, citizens' advisers.
To help with the transitions of retirement	To reproduce some of the rhythms and structures of work.
To learn new skills	Being trained as a Samaritan or becoming a 'wwoofer' and learning organic farming skills (with World Wide Opportunities on Organic Farms).
To use existing skills	Teachers and parents can become school governors; people with professional skills can become trustees; social services carers can join the Royal Voluntary Service (previously known as WRVS) meals-on-wheels service. Volunteering abroad as a 'silver gapper'.
To develop social networks	Volunteering to work in a team and share experiences, meeting people with similar interests.
To explore political interests	Volunteering with an organisation such as a political party, Amnesty International, Reprieve and so on.

What Kind of Volunteering?

Older volunteers are quite particular about what they want to do and what they think they will find worthwhile. There is such a variety of opportunities that they can try out, pick and choose the activities that suit their interests, time commitment, skills, and also what they want to give and receive. Types of task, and examples of what they may involve, can be very varied.

- **Clerical** – photocopying, filing, envelope stuffing, reception work.
- **Befriending** – visiting isolated people, supporting carers.
- **Mentoring** – assisting as 'grandmentors', people over 50 paired

with unemployed young people (a Community Service Volunteers scheme).

- **Information and advice** – offering advice and advocacy in many spheres.
- **Practical tasks** – driving patients to hospital, small DIY projects, gardening.
- **Welfare, therapy, support** – talking to patients, staffing helplines.
- **Trusteeship** – serving on boards, using professional skills with local and national charities.

Not all volunteers choose their activities for the specific tasks they undertake or the skills they use. One volunteer in a homeless persons' shelter explained:

> You might only be serving tea or coffee, but you are doing more than that because sometimes these people come to the counter and they can't carry anything, and you take it to them and see them settled. You're helping that person and that's what it's all about in my eyes, it's helping someone.

Using previous skills is often a strong motivation, and it is valuable to organisations that need but can't afford to employ skilled workers. Retired civil servants, administrators, nurses and teachers take on tasks similar to those with which they were familiar. Trusteeship clearly gains from these skills. Sue is a retired teacher, but has always been active in local amateur dramatics. She uses her dramatic skills and experience to record books for the blind. As a cancer survivor herself, Mavis wanted to help people being treated for cancer and who live abroad. She lives in France and volunteered with an organisation near her home.

Some may want to contribute for a specific period, as was the case with the 2012 London Olympics. A media campaign for volunteers resulted in 240,000 applications from adults of all ages for 70,000 places. Games Makers received no advantages in terms of tickets, but plenty of reward in terms of playing a part in making a big event successful. Many said at interview that they wanted to help make this special event a success. Others wanted to give something back to sports.

Volunteering to support activities in specific areas of interest is common, for example assisting with the running of sporting activities or events. Some people may join in the fun run, but others make themselves useful as a steward or helping on the water station.

Combining volunteering with tourism is increasingly popular and the term 'voluntourism' has been coined to describe this activity. Older people who undertake it have been dubbed Grey or Silver Gappers. There are websites to help those who want to take up this adventurous prospect (see the Resources section at the back of the book for more information). Retirees often have skills that are very useful to organisations overseas (e.g., teaching, project management, planning and designing, healthcare, construction skills). Unlike younger gappers, these retirees don't need to establish themselves in a career and can take advantage of being flexible with their time. But they do share with younger gappers the sense for adventure, the search for a challenge and the desire to experience how others live. And they may want to make a difference.

One such gapper, Heloise Kareem, described her experiences in life-changing terms:

At 70 I am … part of a new generation of retired people, who have spent most of their lives in full-time work but are still healthy and energetic and not ready to settle into a round of bridge parties and evening classes. I was particularly interested in going to Northern India and found an organisation called 'i-to-i' which could offer me two teaching placements of two months each.

My accommodation in Santiniketan was a dream come true – a bungalow set in a garden full of banana and mango trees and singing birds. The main part of my project was to teach English in a small free private school for 80 children from underprivileged homes from pre-school age to ten …

Weeks after returning to London, I am still wondering what to make of it all. I certainly had a stimulating and happy experience and I feel it has had a profound effect on my view of the world. My view of poverty has radically altered. Many older people can offer invaluable experience, which can be of more use than the enthusiasm but inexperience of a teenager.

Similarly, Michael Lowe, a retired managing director, took a two-month retirement 'gap year' in Tanzania with Mondo Challenge Foundation. He worked on a Business Development project, which gives small grants to people suffering from HIV. He said: 'It was a very challenging time, and at the beginning I didn't think I would be able to adapt, but after a couple of weeks I felt like part of the community. There is so much opportunity to help and get involved.'

There are many such stories. Gwen Dale-Jones, a retired teacher, taught in India with Mondo Challenge Foundation. She spent three months in Kalimpong (Darjeeling district, north India) in a local primary school. She said: 'The best words to describe my experience would be truly amazing. I could never believe how quickly the extraordinary experiences I had became the normal way of life so quickly. There was never a dull moment.' And Silvia Russenberger, 66, looked after animals in the Tambotie Wildlife Care Centre, as part of a conservation project with African Conservation Experience.

The stories of these gappers touch on many themes of this book: a desire to be adventurous, to use continued health, energy, skills and experience, to get involved in helping others and develop a new perspective on life as a result.

Other travelling volunteers may not wish to spend time in developing countries, but rather to enjoy more sedate experiences nearer home. In Berlin, for example, in return for expenses and language training, over-50s can volunteer for six weeks to work in educational, not-for-profit and art organisations. The participants connect with people of different generations across cultures (see the Resources section).

Finding the Right Opportunities

Word of mouth is the most common source of information about volunteering activities. Being asked to become involved is one of the strongest factors in encouraging volunteers. This suggests that people may not have a full picture of the possibilities before they choose where to put their efforts. And it explains why they often choose activities where they have a personal connection.

Volunteering agencies are always on the lookout for new volunteers. Recruitment to trustee positions reveals that there is always more demand for trustees than people putting themselves forward. Retirees who have skills and experience in accountancy and legal careers are always in demand to become trustees, but may be unaware of this. Many trustees are recruited through the recommendation of friends. Improved recruitment to trustee positions would bring in trustees from a wider range of sources and encourage retiring professionals to offer their skills and experience. There are many sources of information about availability of trusteeships, including on websites, national and local organisations, and newspaper adverts (see the Resources section).

For all types of formal volunteering, recruitment might be a more satisfactory process if the skills needed and the expectations (e.g., type of activities, time to be given, training) were clearly explained.

Many employing organisations, especially in the public sector, find that members of the workforce are prepared to continue to volunteer their skills, knowledge and wisdom. Jacqui MacDonald, head of staff and organisational development at the Institute of Education, University of London, launched an initiative to get retirees to share their knowledge and expertise to support the professional development of other staff. She says: 'They contribute to retiring workshops, writing support, coaching and mentoring, assisting with drafting research proposals, work shadowing (especially on international travels), facilitating lunchtime or end-of-day workshops and supporting staff with promotion applications.' The initiative is also a way of reducing ageism in the workplace, she added.

If you are considering volunteering, ask yourself:

1. What aspects of my life (inside and outside work) provide the most satisfaction?
2. What am I most passionate about?
3. Who have I enjoyed working with and why?
4. Do I want to volunteer my time on a regular or ad hoc basis?
5. What skills do I want to continue to use?
6. What new skills would I like to develop?
7. What would I like to spend time doing?
8. What interests do I pursue at the moment?
9. What important areas in my life would I want to keep?
10. In what ways are my ambitions for volunteering in retirement similar to my ambitions in my working life, or am I perhaps interested in a completely different role?

Once you are clearer about what kind of volunteering activity may suit you, your next task may be to make some enquiries in the local library or search online and see what's available in your local area.

Commitment and Responsibilities

Volunteering activities and employment may share some attributes, especially if the choice of activity has been motivated by the desire to ease the transition from work. Where an organisation has invested in the training of volunteers and where it needs to plan using skilled personnel, it may seek a commitment. This might be for a certain number of hours, for a certain length of time, and with a specified period of notice. Volunteers may require further training and periodic reviews. Where a team is involved there will be responsibilities to others, including other volunteers. And if volunteers are being paid expenses (e.g., for driving patients to hospital), they need to be ready to complete the necessary paperwork.

There are implications for trustees and these too need to be clear. The Charity Commission website www.charitycommission.gov.uk provides a good guide to the risks and implications.

Benefits to the Community

There is a great deal of discussion about the cost of older people, as if they make no financial or social contributions. People over 65 put more into the economy than they take out, in economic terms, according to the 'Gold Age Pensioners' report by the Royal Voluntary Service (previously known as WRVS). The report estimates that currently older people contribute about £40bn more to the economy than they cost. This contribution is made in a number of ways, in particular through volunteering. Older people provide 104.6 hours per year of informal volunteering (e.g., caring for family members and neighbours), worth £34bn per annum, and growing to an estimated £127bn in 2030. They also provide 54.5 hours per year of formal volunteering with a charity, worth £10bn per annum.

And of course older people provide more than an economic dividend, especially while providing informal and formal voluntary services. The 'Gold Age Pensioners' report refers to this, rather inelegantly, as 'social glue'. It explains that older people play an important role in encouraging neighbourliness, providing useful skills and experiences, offering advocacy and leadership, promoting local security, and generally being pillars of the community through their active participation. Moreover, as active users of local services they ensure that services are provided.

Appreciation of their contribution comes from Sir Stephen Bubb, chief executive of the Association of Chief Executives of Voluntary Organisations, who has identified three ways in which the voluntary sector benefits as a result. First, older people's contribution provides social gain, or public benefit, which enriches lives and communities, 'from installing IT infrastructure to getting stuck in redeveloping your local environment'. Second, older people provide much valued and needed skills and experience (e.g., professional people have skills required to become trustees). Finally, older people can nurture the potential for leadership in younger participants, through peer mentoring. Bubb sees older people's advantages to society as transforming the narrative of ageing from dependence to participation.

Interests

Some people would use the word hobby here, but it suggests a lack of seriousness, a sideline, a diversion, a fad, something frivolous, and does not reflect the commitment, passion and depth that retirees bring to what they do. Undertaking leisure and cultural activities is the most frequently mentioned aspiration for later life, according to the Department for Work & Pensions. Many people look forward to and enjoy being able to immerse themselves in their interests when they have more time. They follow established interests and become involved in new activities. In addition to the intrinsic pleasures, spending time on your interests brings people together and can create new or stronger social connections, provide purpose and structure to time. In short, it's good for your health and general well-being.

Making music appears to be especially beneficial to individual and group enjoyment. Musicians aged 50–93 were found to have more positive relationships and a brighter outlook, and derived more pleasure than those in less creative activities, according to a report in the *Telegraph* titled 'Making Music the Key to Happy Retirement'. They believed that they had improved concentration and memory as a result of their musical activities.

You could also gain the additional satisfaction of earning money from pursuing your interests, for example by dealing in antiques, making and selling craft items or trading online in stocks and shares.

Many working people prepare for a time when they will be more able to enjoy their interests. They subscribe to relevant magazines, or become relatively inactive members of relevant organisations, keeping in touch if not actively involved. They stock up on expensive kit, such as tapestry materials. It's another way of thinking ahead and being prepared for the increased available time.

Others say that on retiring they are going to spend a few months deciding what they want to do and see which way their interests evolve.

Formal Education

Learning to adapt to the changes of retirement can be described as informal learning. This section focuses on formal learning. There are many opportunities for formal learning, including courses online, such as those offered by the Open University, which can be a godsend to those who are housebound or need to study at idiosyncratic times. Many retirees enjoy the experience of attending classes organised locally by the Workers' Educational Association or their local education authority, or by the University of the Third Age. Many courses are specifically for the over-60s, but there are plenty of opportunities for people who want to mix with adults of all ages.

Bertie Gladwin graduated at 90 with an MA in Intelligence History. His account in the *Guardian* of his experiences suggests an admirable combination of formal and informal learning:

> My higher education formally began when I was in my 60s (I left school at 14 in 1935), as I had not previously had an opportunity to study before my retirement and the advent of the wonderful Open University. But long before then, first working in the Temple as a barrister's clerk, and then joining the wartime RAF, my eyes were opened to a broader culture than that offered by my south-east London street. An innate curiosity and a seemingly insatiable thirst for knowledge accounted for the rest. In short, I have come late to formal higher education, but have lived a lifetime of learning.

Jane likes learning new skills in an area not directly connected with her previous employment in teaching. She is enrolled on an MA course, studying International Development. She is one of thousands. By 2004 there were more than 600,000 signed up to formal classes in England alone. The University of the Third Age had 140,000 attendees. Every year more than 5,000 people aged 65 and over are registered on courses at the Open University.

Many people have strong internal voices that reject the idea of formal learning. This is a response to experiences of the education system 50 or more years ago, especially if it involved failure and fear. An established and successful secondary head teacher revealed to his teaching staff that he had loved singing in his primary school choir. But when a concert approached, the teacher took him aside and suggested that he mime singing because his voice was so awful. He has never sung a note since. He told the story to demonstrate how strong the impact of teachers' criticisms can be. Family attitudes can also influence attitudes to learning.

The experience of formal education in schools was often dismal because one way or another its purpose was to get information in people's heads. Rote learning of disconnected facts, such as the names and dates of the kings and queens of England, was a dreary task. Such activities never had a useful purpose and have been rendered completely unnecessary by the accessibility of all kinds of information in books and on the internet. But the experience goes deep and an inability to reproduce information is linked with failure and stupidity in people's minds. A common experience of learning has been to give up in the face of difficulties, and many approaching retirement will adopt this outlook. It is the legacy of the British education system for many of those reaching retirement now. But in retirement this reluctance to learn can be overcome. Courses and classes are designed to be very accessible to older people who have not studied for some time. Even in formal settings, classes are informal and can be great fun. Going to such a class with a friend may appeal to you and will get over the wariness that you might feel.

The idea of taking an exam or some other form of assessment may put you off, especially if you thought you had finished with examinations 40 years earlier, or if you are making a tentative foray into formal education perhaps after a gap of decades. So you might want to check out the courses that do not have assessment.

Other circumstances may limit your access to formal learning, such as location, travel, finance or health. Or you may have anxieties about safety and security leaving home. There may also be an anxiety about feeling left out when joining a group, and of not knowing what to do or what to say in a class. That's when a friend or family member can provide support.

Government policy for so-called lifelong learning equates life with employment unfortunately, and does not fund courses for those considered to be economically inactive, such as retirees. However, many retirees want to enjoy opportunities to learn, and some are able and prepared to spend money on these themselves. And some retirees are prepared to teach on these courses.

An inner voice might be repeating the phrase about the impossibility of teaching old dogs new tricks but Ellen's experience is a good counter-argument. On retiring from her work in the NHS four years ago, Ellen wanted to learn three new things: to swim, to drive and to play the piano. She has achieved the first two and is now considering how to achieve the third, worried about the possible disturbance to her neighbours of her inexperienced practising. In the meantime she has joined a choir to help her learn music. She plans to negotiate to use a piano in a nearby church hall. She is an example of the many retirees who want to grasp the opportunities for new learning that retiring offers.

It is often a specific challenge or impetus that spurs people on to their learning projects. For Ellen it was the availability of spare time to devote to her three ambitions. For Jim Kelly, 84, it was his granddaughter Becky's frustration with his inability to answer her questions. 'Don't you know anything, Grandad?' she said. He signed up 14 years ago for classes on a whole range of topics, including gardening and history, and in 2010 he won the Adult Learner's Week Award.

Others, however, and this may well be you, will choose not to sign up to formal education. As Bertie Gladwin claims, we live a lifetime of learning. Outside the formal education system of schools, colleges and universities, with their assessment systems, most adults are successful learners, without acknowledging this capacity. After all, you probably learned to drive, to use a mobile phone and computer, developed skills at work, and dealt with demanding situations in your private life. You are already an expert at learning.

Holidays

Why on earth would you want to go on holidays when retired? Aren't you on a perpetual holiday? It may surprise you to find that you may still need holidays – for the change of climate, scenery and routine; the fun; to marvel at new places; for the company if you live alone; for a break from caring for others; in fulfilment of a dream; or for the enjoyment of the activities and culture that are involved. There is a huge advantage in the opportunity of taking holidays outside the peak times of school holidays when they are cheaper and more peaceful. Your holidays can last for longer than previously, and this can mean travelling to destinations further afield. Caroline's friend Archie planned to visit all the people on his Christmas card list within the first two years of his retirement. As you contemplate retirement, think about the holidays you will be able to enjoy.

Doing Nothing Very Much

Retired people are supposed to keep very busy and active. Inactivity in retirement is frequently described in judgmental ways. The message is that you have a responsibility, a duty in retirement, to be mentally and physically active. Sometimes this is even coupled with the idea that you should pay something back for the pensions you receive, as if they haven't been paid for already during working life and through taxes. But there are people, and you may be one of them, for whom doing nothing very much is what you want after a lifetime of labour, for a short while, or perhaps forever.

It is widely assumed that a fulfilling life requires purpose and meaning. This may not be true for everyone though, psychology research found in 2010. About two-thirds of the people involved in this research did want meaning and purpose in their lives. However, another 30 per cent did not experience life as meaningful and they did not suffer from the lack of meaning either.

An unsurprising detail in this study was that being unemployed is related to a lack of meaning for some people. However, people receiving pensions did not suffer in the same way as the unemployed. Many of them were fully occupied and did not see themselves as unemployed, even if they didn't have a job. A significant proportion of these people, from 19 per cent to 38 per cent, were indifferent to the idea of purpose in their lives – the researcher called them the 'existentially indifferent'. If these figures are reproduced across the retired population of the UK, then about a quarter (28 per cent) of potential readers of this book have little desire to make their lives meaningful. They are happily existentially indifferent! There may be many people in retirement who do not want purposeful and meaningful occupation. And it may be that other people may experience periods of time when they do not feel the need for meaning or purpose either, and that's just fine.

Closing Thoughts

It is no longer the case that retirement is the waiting room for death, the last stage of life. There is so much to do, so many activities to enjoy, so many opportunities for volunteering, and so many holidays to plan, look forward to and enjoy.

Retirement is an opportunity to enjoy a life of richness, to shape your life so that it includes more interests, more service to others, more adventure. Be bold, be brave, surprise yourself and have lots of fun while you're at it.

Chapter 6

A Little Help from My Friends?

Remember the Beatles' song 'Oh, I get by with a little help from my friends'? We could all do with some support at important moments in our lives, especially during the turbulent period of change after leaving work. It may come as a surprise to you that the changes and transitions of retiring can last for several years. Encouragement, challenge and validation are vital when considering your choices and making decisions. Support networks and social connections provide both informal and formal help.

Family, friends and religion are often identified as the main sources of support to retirees. But talking through issues of confusion about leaving work, ambivalence about being retired, changes to your image and difficulties in relationships may be more effectively discussed with other people, especially with other retirees who are going through similar experiences as yourself. Reciprocal arrangements of support are particularly beneficial.

This chapter examines the case for support, and how to find help. Two recurring themes emerge. One, as women form the majority in support groups and coaching it is clear that gender strongly influences attitudes to seeking support; men are not expected to discuss or show their feelings as much. An explanation for this division is provided by Geert Hofstede, a Dutch researcher and social psychologist who claims that in 'masculine' cultures men are expected to be ambitious and competitive. 'Feminine' cultures are more collective because personal relationships are more significant to women. Women care more for the non-material quality of life than men, and value talking about their situations with other women.

Two, levels of education, income and class position are related to seeking professional support outside the family. These factors determine the choices and options. For those who like theoretical explanations, Pierre Bourdieu refers to this as 'social capital' – resources people achieve through group membership, relationships, networks of influence, and support from other people.

The Case for Support

Retiring and retirement take much longer to move through than you might imagine. Social, practical and emotional factors intertwine, making it a complex process. You will experience some form of adjustment after you leave work, although your feelings may differ in duration from another person's and could vary in intensity.

An individual's support needs differ during the zones of pre-retirement, retiring and retirement. The more preparation, the better – this helps counter the feeling of 'entering a void'. Three examples from our workshops confirm this.

- The decisions taken before retiring may partly determine how people adjust to the next phases. Joan said, 'Facing up to my financial situation was hard but I got a good sense of what was going to happen.'
- Support increases the ability to find successful ways through unfamiliar territory. Martha said, 'I am thinking of all those groups and networks I can get support from when I am no longer at work.'
- Working with a coach to envision life when work is not the centre

of a retiree's life is extremely valuable. Caroline said a visualising exercise 'has confirmed my general vision for my future …'.

You may feel a mixture of relief, loss, even depression or disorientation in the retiring phase. The process may be similar to grieving. You will be losing several important components in your life: work, routine, a professional self-image, community, friendships and a sense of control. Like bereavement there may be a yearning for the past, a desire for the confusion to end and a need to get on with life. The longing to be back at work may continue for a considerable time. Chris and Frank who are in their 80s still miss the social aspects of work, especially when it's cold and dark. They love being outdoors, but gardening, exploring and visiting friends are not as enjoyable in winter.

Old ways of thinking and acting are changed: you will need to let go of the familiar. Talking through the meaning of change and loss, through coaching or in workshops, can help. This requires a readiness and openness to learn. Retirees may find such explorations difficult as it can expose vulnerabilities. This may relate to the gender and class issues flagged up earlier.

Following 'disorientation' comes reorientation and a time for learning about *who* you want to be now that you're retired. You may then feel more at ease. You may become wiser, and more in tune with your body and spiritual self. Jennifer, one member of our retiring group, described such a transformation as the opportunity to adopt a slower and less stressful way of life in which she responds to her body's natural rhythms, such as getting up and going to bed when she needs to, not when work dictates, spending more time with her family, growing vegetables and fruit on her allotment which she cooks with her grandchildren. All these activities bring her closer to her family and wider community.

Support and pleasure can be found in a variety of ways, as in creative groups. We have noticed that when moving through transitions some people start artistic projects. The relaxed atmosphere is often ideal for discussing and sharing ideas around retirement.

Men and women often find friendship and enjoyment when they engage in sport, and people sometimes seek the additional support of a personal trainer. Work with the body is often neglected in our busy working lives and retirement is a great time to reintegrate body and mind.

Specific Help with Changes and Transitions

Finding support for your decision to retire is the first task. The decision is often complicated as it may affect a number of other people and will almost certainly determine your financial situation for the rest of your life. Assessing reasons to leave work or stay, anticipating the effects of changing work patterns, when and how to go are some dilemmas to resolve.

The notion of 'career reorientation' is also useful. It suggests that retirees need the same self-analysis that they gave to every other stage of their career. Our former colleague Jacqui MacDonald, head of staff and organisational development at the Institute of Education, University of London, agrees – the best practices in planning for retiring are precisely those that are important for any other stage in professional development. In her account in *Retiring Lives* she states that all organisations have the responsibility to provide support for individuals who are contemplating changes to their working lives. That is why she is so supportive of pre-retirement workshops.

In the pre-retirement workshops that we run, people are keen to discuss:

- what's important in life and work at present, and how to find replacements – continuities and discontinuities;
- what they will lose and gain in their transitions;
- the social aspects of retirement, such as finding new communities; and
- stories from veteran retirees about how they managed and survived.

In the immediate period after leaving work, support is needed for making changes and understanding ambivalent feelings. Financial support is advisable and other specialist advice may be appropriate when considering the advantages and drawbacks of moving abroad, setting up a new business, working as a freelance consultant. Later on, support is needed to: review the effects of the decisions you have made and the changes to a new way of life; develop a new image and new roles; and think about preferred retirement situations.

An analysis of the history of a women's retiring group highlights important themes and can be used in two ways – one, to provide inspiration for group discussion topics; two, for you as an individual to reflect on your changing situation.

A checklist for thinking about changes in retirement
Attending to the different dimensions of your life beyond work, such as:
- ❏ finding intellectual stimulation;
- ❏ returning to part-time work or consultancy;
- ❏ extending your friendships;
- ❏ caring for your physical, spiritual and social well-being;
- ❏ uncovering emotional and creative expression;
- ❏ becoming politically involved; and
- ❏ volunteering.

Leaving work and the organisation behind, such as:
- ❏ taking charge of the process of leaving;
- ❏ considering the issues in letting go; and
- ❏ ensuring that the ending or endings are appropriate.

Reflecting on what you value in your life, such as:
- ❏ constructing a purpose in retirement;
- ❏ questioning the need to be useful; and
- ❏ making a contribution.

Making sense of the process of retiring, such as:

- ❑ understanding there will be many different transitions;
- ❑ making sense of a new kind of life;
- ❑ developing an identity as a retiree, reinventing and changing identities;
- ❑ seeing retiring as a process, not an event; and
- ❑ welcoming change.

Getting support in challenging times, such as:

- ❑ grieving for a loss and coping with depression and illness;
- ❑ separating from loved ones, dealing with loss and family crisis;
- ❑ accepting ageing and your changing feelings about becoming older; and
- ❑ dealing with ageism and the negative views and behaviour of others.

Setting goals and making plans, such as:

- ❑ anticipating and preparing for life with further challenges;
- ❑ reviewing the previous year;
- ❑ making detailed or tentative plans for the next months and years;
- ❑ finding ways to fulfil your dreams; and
- ❑ having fun.

Sources of Support

You may wish to consider a range of options in order to find the right type of support at the right time. Some prefer face-to-face support, others enjoy the anonymity of the internet, many like planned and formal settings, others informal or spontaneous situations. Some like groups; others don't. Reading and researching is fruitful for some. Over the periods of pre-retirement, retiring and retirement, you may draw on different forms of support at different times and even at the same time.

The Advantages of Belonging to a Self-Help Group

Self-help groups run on common principles: members participate with the expectation of receiving support, they disclose personal experiences and find ways to manage shared problems. This is why they often appeal to women. These are grassroots organisations – developed and run by their members. One of their empowering features is that members experience autonomy, control of the group, and a sense that they are experts on their problems. For example, some retiring groups do not arrange for experts to discuss finance, health or other practical issues. They draw on their own resources and strength in their collective wisdom.

In the retirement support group mentioned earlier to which we both belong, eight women from the same organisation set up their group in order to build a community of people who share the same focus and values. There were strong social connections within the group. All of us had people we count as friends among the members when we joined.

We decided to meet regularly, and expected members to make a commitment to a regular period of time, usually meeting once a month. We were aware that the amount of time it takes to travel to and from the group increased the demand on group members. Some had further to travel than others. At first we met in our organisation, then gradually as people felt disconnected to the workplace we met in people's houses or cafes.

While we managed the group ourselves, we benefited from having a facilitator for our first residential experience. From then on we relied on the skills of the group members.

The group developed its social cohesion through residential weekends, through joint (but not exclusive) activities such as walking together, dining, sharing experiences of books, films, writing and numerous other valuable bits of information (poems, recipes, underwear shops, websites and so forth), and – everyone's favourite – cocktails. One of the members, Anne Gold, observed that:

The Retiring Women's group helped me by providing a space dedicated to thinking about issues and to hearing other people planning and talking. If I hadn't reflected on retirement and tried to make sense of it, it would have hit me quite painfully. Having a dedicated space where I could hear other people's stories was important. Also our time together allowed me to realise that there were a couple of things that I wanted to do on retirement, and that I have done – that realisation came through thinking and talking in the group ... The other thing is that the group has given me permission not to do anything some days, so I can sit and read – just to go slower.

Issues Arising from the Retiring Women's Group and Other Retiring Groups

The success of the women's group described above is evidenced by the fact that it's still running after six years, indicating that it is meeting the changing needs of its members and that individuals are committed to making the group work. During its six years much interest has been shown, including by the BBC Radio 4 *Woman's Hour* in May 2010. The problem the group has now is finding a time when all members can attend, as their lives are so diverse. One member is working full-time again, others part-time, one lives abroad, several are engaged in voluntary work and other activities, while some have responsibility for grandchildren. From its inception other colleagues and friends wanted to join. The group remained closed to new members as it was felt that a larger group would be unmanageable, less effective and it would be difficult to absorb new members after the group had become cohesive. Subsequently, new mixed groups of men and women were set up in that organisation.

Situated in one organisation it is good to have a safe and confidential place where members can discuss emergent issues. Other groups are formed where members come from different workplaces and may not have known each other previously. Both arrangements have advantages and drawbacks.

All eight members of our group were experienced in working collectively in teams. However, there were some criticisms of how the group functioned. For example, one member felt the experience could have been more challenging. She suspected that being a professor gave her licence to talk as if she knew how to prepare for retirement, rather than be questioned about her boundaries and priorities. This indicates that different power positions restrict learning. Other groups use facilitators. Their role is to encourage individuals to make power dynamics explicit, learn from their experiences and change the way the group operates. This is important as some group members can feel excluded when discussion takes place around issues that don't affect them, such as having grandchildren, being in a partnership, or a discussion on books or films that they have not read or seen. It's important not to alienate members by ignoring their needs, being insensitive to their situation or assuming some issues will be relevant to all. Reviewing the function of the group and its effectiveness at regular intervals is crucial for survival.

The strength of a group is that it provides validation – supporting people in making changes. We have found that groups can be very effective in providing support, challenging and extending group members' learning. They provide a network or community that is rich in support, social trust and information and which helps give members the resources they need to achieve their goals.

For some women it's important to be part of a single-sex group, as Anne Gold explains. When she is exploring her feelings and what oppresses and empowers her, she needs freedom to feel and think. Others find that they want the diverse richness of a mixed group.

Men-only groups exist, but are fewer in number. One such group, in which all the participants were senior managers taking early retirement, took part in a research project. Their experiences were described in an article entitled 'The Experience of Retirement in Second Modernity'. One member of that group explained:

A friend of mine rang me up (this was about seven years ago) and said he's inviting a group of six people, including myself, to agree to meet as a men's group to talk about retirement. And we eventually did that, six of us ... And we met for about five years, during which time we all went through, as I put it, 'to the other side' – you know how people talk about death! (laughs). And I remember the first one to get to the other side, and we said, 'What's it like on the other side?!' And it did feel like that; it's quite an interesting metaphor. And we're all on the other side now, we've all survived it, we're all alive, and the group sort of ran out of an agenda about a year or so ago, so it doesn't meet any more, but we know each other socially.

'The other side' is a powerful metaphor used to convey a strong and dark transition, something approaching a death-like experience. These men found the transition challenging and they provide evidence of the need for continued support over several years.

The two groups discussed here were very successful in meeting the individual members' needs. Their social class, levels of education and financial resources appear highly significant in their ability to make choices. For example:

- they are well off financially, have good pensions and are mainly in good health;
- their retirements are either before or around 65, which allows them to have a positive view of the next stages of their lives;
- they make conscious efforts to prepare for their retirement in a deliberate way and use the group to support their planning process;
- they share the same values;
- their confidence gained from their backgrounds and previous working experiences allows them to participate in groups to examine personal issues; and
- they understand they can take different paths into retirement and so have high expectations for this phase of life.

These factors highlight that a range of choices may not be available to less privileged people. The long-standing support arising from these groups plays a crucial role in these retirees' lives. The success of groups requires a high level of commitment from each member, reciprocity, equity, knowledge and interpersonal skills.

Finding Group Support Online

The flexibility and anonymity of internet groups may appeal to you if you do not enjoy face-to-face experiences or are unable to travel easily. The fact that email lists can function as communities, with their own cultural norms, is well established; members expect to read about others' experiences in dealing with common issues. Internet self-help groups are available 24 hours a day and are free. Members can access social, practical and emotional support whenever they like, for periods of time that suit their existing commitments and as frequently as required. Every imaginable issue around retirement is served by thousands of self-help groups. Some are very active, generating 50 or more messages a day.

Health seems to be a very popular focus of internet groups such as the Healthy Ageing & Retirement Support Group. There are different types of groups available, including: the retirement transition group, the retirement and divorce group, or for those born in a particular decade there are the 1930s, 40s, 50s groups, and retired pen pals.

The advantages of online groups are that:

- they are open;
- they are available to everyone at any time and people can leave whenever they want;
- members are not required to fulfil an active role but can be 'listeners';
- there are few rules; and
- there are different developmental levels that take account of retirees' experiences.

Unlike face-to-face retirement groups discussed earlier, there is little evidence to show the effectiveness of online support. But the popularity of such groups suggests they are useful and appeal to a wide range of people regardless of their class or level of income.

Coaching

Coaching – paying a qualified 'life coach' to work through some issues with you in a one-to-one setting – can provide a helpful bridge in supporting retirees through their transitions when they may be handling complex, ambivalent and disorienting dilemmas. In a period of transition people are often faced with questions, the need to evaluate the structures that currently support them and the need to look for new possibilities. This period may have distinctive tasks, including gaining a new perspective on one's life.

Activities that are particularly helpful in coaching include exploring resistance to change, examining ambivalence and visualising the future. Caroline describes the helpfulness of such a process:

> I re-engaged with 'backward planning' recently. I was practising skills with some fellow work coaches and we were again invited to consider how we wanted our life to be five years ahead. Then we visualised three years ahead, then one, then six months. The final step was to plan what needed to be done between each stage. I have just come through my first six months, which has done two important things. First it has confirmed my general vision for my future in five years' time, and also given me a sense of achievement as I have made considerable progress with the practical things I need to do to achieve the life I want. Now as I move into my second six-month period, I review the overall direction, and then the interim plans. The major shift is that I intend to finish paid work at my institution sooner than in the first plan.

The value of coaching is the focus it provides in resolving complicated issues. It's unlikely that retirees would experience such a structured activity in any other setting, such as a conversation with a friend. Spending an uninterrupted hour concentrating on one issue with a professional coach is a powerful experience. Our friend Diana thought that some support would have been helpful at one stage when she was unable to be systematic about changing her practices or how she thought about herself. She said, 'A personal coach might have buoyed me up, made me see that things would not go on as before and kept me on track.' Retirees can achieve a purposeful and fulfilling retirement with a coach who supports their planning process.

Coaching may be useful for you as it provides an opportunity to examine the questions that you are facing, and will give you the chance to reappraise your current situation before looking to the future.

Courses

Workers who have given serious time and thought to life after retiring will generally experience a smoother transition than those who have not. That's why so many organisations offer courses. Check out what might be available to you. Ashley, another colleague in his 60s, attended a pre-retirement course. His account highlights the benefits:

A key moment in the period leading up to retirement was attending a retirement course … It proved to be a well-organised, useful and enjoyable day. About 20 people attended (all approaching retirement) and there were some interesting whole group and small group discussions. Sharing of experience permeated the day and the overall feeling I left with was that I was not unlike many people at the same stage of life and that I was ahead of many in my thinking about and preparing for retirement. The organisers, recent retirees who had set up a business running such courses, provided full documentation incorporating a lot of useful contact addresses and possibilities.

Ashley was ahead of others in his thinking, which confirms a general lack of planning in middle age. Life Academy is a well-known provider of courses across the UK for individuals or organisations that do not have their own in-house provision (see the Resources section).

Courses are not only about finance, although that does seem to be their main thrust. An analysis of online information on a range of courses and seminars shows that advice about state benefits, occupational and personal pensions, taxation, income and capital gains tax, inheritance tax and will planning outstripped the other themes of adjustment to retirement, life after work, opportunities for voluntary and paid work, leisure activities, health and fitness. It is good to have help on finance but there is so much more to consider.

One problem with retirement courses is that they are designed for the pre-retirement phase. People often go at the last minute and have insufficient time to prepare for the course, and may therefore not benefit fully from the experience. Decisions about retirement are made over a long period of time and a one-day course is unlikely to be satisfactory. You may find that if a course is limited to one day there may be unresolved issues for you and other forms of support may be needed.

Informal Support from Friends and Family

The family may be your most cherished community – the value of being part of one is evidenced throughout this book. There are huge benefits of supportive inter-generational living, caring for and being cared for by parents, children and grandchildren. The significance of partners as a source of emotional, practical and social support is evident by the huge impact of their loss. Children can also take on a key support role, especially as parents become older and are less able to look after themselves.

Your friends or family members can fulfil many of the functions described in this chapter. They can help arrange and attend your retirement party (if you have one), provide support during the years of transition, and act as your informal coach. Friendship networks can be crucial in your life, especially if you have few close family members around. It may be useful to spend time with friends who are close in age to you and are experiencing changes themselves. During challenging periods, informal conversations that compare reactions are a great source of encouragement.

Closing Thoughts

A successful and fulfilling retirement requires ongoing support. You will need help when making the decision to leave work, for early adjustments and for further periods of change. It is important to try out different approaches in order to find those that suit you best. Retirees who belong to social networks and communities rich in support are able to access vital resources, which help them make retirement enjoyable and rewarding. So it is worth exploring networks that already exist or setting up a new group with a little help from your friends.

Chapter 7

Could-you-just?
Communicating with
Family and Friends

Relationships with family and friends will change in retirement as you have more available time. It's not always easy to manage this time or the expectations other people have of how you will use it. Tensions may emerge in these changing relationships and effective communication is crucial, especially the need to be clear about your own plans and priorities. Partners and friends, seeing you as constantly available, ask, '*Could you just* ... pick up the dry-cleaning, iron a shirt ...', which you may find infuriating.

The chapter probes into these potential areas of discontent and looks at how you can manage them.

Sources of Tension and Conflict

Your life will change in retirement in many ways and some changes will come as a bit of a shock to you, your partners, friends and families. Personal and marital relationships become scrutinised. Tensions may be inevitable.

Different tensions arise according to different circumstances. You and your partner might be adjusting to life as a retired couple, or one of you might still be working with the other recently retired. Or you might have to deal with the issues arising from one partner returning to work after you have both retired.

Vera's story represents the first scenario, with both partners adapting to their retirement together:

> We retired from full-time jobs at roughly the same time, five years ago. Graham, my husband still gets under my feet and he's always looking for things to do. He comes into my kitchen when I'm preparing meals and I don't like it. He complains when my friends come round and feels he can't stay in the house. He goes to his shed where he potters doing God knows what. He helped decorate our daughter's flat but ended up in casualty when he fell off a ladder above the stairwell onto his head. I thought he was done for but he survived. He's now cutting the hedge up a stepladder with an electric saw. I tell him he's too old at 70. He said, 'How do you know when you are too old to go up ladders?' I have loads to do and am never bored but Graham has never had hobbies. I think he's lonely. He has no real friends now he's stopped working. We don't do much together and seem to bicker a lot.

Three points are particularly striking from Vera's story. One, it takes years to adjust to retirement and many compromises need to be made. Some people say that it's like getting married all over again. After years at work when couples only see each other in the morning and evening, it comes as a bit of a surprise when both partners retire and spend all day – every day – together. This may be even more difficult when the children have left home and when there may be a gradual realisation that couples have little in common.

Two, entrenched gender roles are limiting and stifling. Difficulties in adjusting to retirement stem from loss of status and identity associated with leaving paid work, mainly for men whose careers may be seen as more important, and when retirees have been strongly attached to their work. Women may find retirement less stressful as they may be more adaptable and have more interests. For example, they may find it easier to adjust as they may be looking after grand-children or occupying themselves with many interesting creative activities and looking after their home and family, whereas if men leave paid work without other interests, they may become quite lost. We are optimistic that this gender division may be less distinct in the next generation.

Three, sharing space can be a nightmare as retirees start to occupy their home in a different way. Vera claims the kitchen as her terri-tory. Graham retreats to his shed. The lesson for you is that you need to negotiate ways of living with others in the space you have avail-able. If you are lucky enough to have a large space, having your own room for dedicated interests might prevent bloodshed and provide a place to escape and be uninterrupted.

The problem of adjusting to retirement is widespread. Many examples emerge. A letter in the *Guardian* Family section in November 2010, from a disgruntled wife to her newly retired husband, includes the following statement of exasperation:

I know I am being unreasonable and I'm sure you must be hating me. I try to reason with myself and remind myself that you live [here] too. It's just that you live here more than me now. I miss my on-my-own-times. I didn't realise how precious they were for my sanity. I don't like this retirement business at all!

And another woman asks an agony aunt in *Saga* magazine:

Now that my husband has retired we have more time to be together, but it's getting me down. He follows me round the house, asks me what I'm doing, quite often tells me how I ought to be doing it. It's absolutely maddening because I've been running the house perfectly well for years. How can I get him to leave me alone?

The insightful agony aunt intimates that her husband is trying to make her fill the place once occupied by his colleagues and exert control like he did at work. You may be troubled by the suggestion that it's women who need to sort men out by finding them things to do – such as volunteering, sport, a course to provide a new interest, cooking or gardening. 'I quite understand why you want to throttle him, but you'll have to help him adjust or you'll go crazy,' the agony aunt said.

The assumption that it's the role of women to help men adjust needs to be challenged – why should they? These gender positions are unhealthy for women and men.

However, it's not all bad news. In one study, on men and women's adjustments to retirement, it was found that most couples reported an overall increase in intimacy after an initial period of adjustment, but the sharing of household tasks and changes in the power balance of relationships are critical issues that can cause serious problems. This problem may intensify if couples adopt conflicting gender identities, or if men stick to traditional views about employment. In most cases, however, this is resolved through dialogue and negotiation.

If you are in a partnership, now is the time for you to re-examine your role in retirement so that you can challenge stereotypical behaviour and attitudes. The freedom of not working gives opportunities to alter how you live your lives, how you spend time together and how you develop new identities.

Mary's story shows the problems that can arise when one partner has retired and the other continues to work:

My partner Rita is ten years older than me. When she retired I still needed to work. At first I felt resentful as I thought she would have more time to do the things I wanted her to do, like the cooking and ironing. Rita is busier now. I didn't expect her to be out so much in the evenings as well as during the days. I thought we would have more evenings together.

I felt excluded from her retiring group. And when we are with friends who are also retired I feel left out when they are talking about organising tickets to go to concerts and other things. I'm doing a full-time job with imposed tasks while others create their own timetable.

After three years of getting used to the situation my view is beginning to change. Now I can see the benefits of all the activities my partner is involved in, seeing she has a more enjoyable life. Our relationship has evolved and so I'm less resentful.

When Rita first retired I thought she would spend more time outside London which is what she'd planned. For both of us that has taken time to realise. So when we both go to the country at weekends and on holiday that feels like our time. That feels less compartmentalised.

We both have new routines and that means our relationship is as equal as ever. I now know her daily routine, like going to the gym first thing. I have my routine where I go to work. I think that our holidays, how we plan and execute them, are a more important part of our life than I thought they would be. That's the time we talk about important things.

But Rita has more energy since she stopped working and that is exhausting for me. She does loads of things and I don't do that much. It is that old cliché that you do more when you are retired. I have to pace myself so that I'm fit for work. I can't do late nights midweek. My work is an important part of who I am. Rita is more disciplined and without the constrictions of a job she is more motivated to do the things she wants. She does activities because she wants to. I work because I have to.

What's worth noting in this scenario? One, pangs of envy may be felt on both sides if one partner is at work and the other isn't. When work is an important part of one partner's life this may cause the other to feel less important, inferior and even lonely. The retiree may feel they don't have an important role or purpose, and may feel the need to create a new identity. The person at work may be hugely resentful of the free time and fun the other is experiencing, not to mention how energetic they may be. They may also feel excluded from activities that take place during the working day when they are not free.

Two, the partner who is still in work needs to be aware that retirees have their own goals and ambitions. Assumptions about how retirees spend their time can lead to conflict. Even in same-sex partnerships antagonism may arise between partners when the retiree is expected to take on more domestic roles. For the working partner it's important that the retiree's new purpose in life is not seen to be about attending to their needs. The mantra of 'Could you just …' can become more and more annoying over time. The expectation that one person is always going to be responsible for looking after the other's needs can lead to deep resentment.

Three, relationships evolve and grow stronger if people talk together and resolve differences. Regular time without distractions, devoted to clearing up misunderstandings and tensions, is important. For Mary and Rita this helped their relationship develop and remain equal, although what they do in their lives is very different.

The implication is clear. If you are in a difficult situation you may want to take Mary's advice and talk with your partner to resolve differences before they become too problematic.

Finally, Pierre's story highlights some of the problems that can arise when one partner decides to return to work after both have retired:

My wife Sabine retired from her work as a translator when she was 60. I ran a garden centre and loved it. I was very happy. I loved the work, the companionship and working outside. Sabine put pressure on me to retire as she wanted us to spend more time together and to go back to France for long holidays. So after two years I gave in and decided to leave work so that I could be with Sabine. I could see that both us of being retired would have several advantages. At first we spent more time in France and I gradually got used to the idea of being retired and I spent time working on my own garden.

A year later Sabine was offered a new contract for an exciting job as a simultaneous translator in Brussels. She jumped at the chance, of course, and took the post. I was very angry as she didn't consult me. I wouldn't have resigned from my job if I thought that Sabine was going to return to work. Now I am living alone most of the time, without the status of work and companionship. I am bored and frustrated.

This is an unusual scenario, but has lessons for all retirees. First, putting pressure on another to retire is a recipe for disaster. This is not an effective way to make decisions about retirement. Second, a most infuriating aspect is the lack of consultation when making a decision that will affect both partners, in this case about returning to work. Third, when a person loses status, the work they are passionate about, their colleagues, income and then the company of a partner, a severe strain is put on a relationship.

These stories reveal the significance of some important principles: trust, equality, openness, respect, control, autonomy, decision-making and patterns of communication.

In light of these case studies, you may wish to review how you make decisions, either those that you make on your own or those you make with other people. These decisions can be about all aspects of your life. In the act of review and discussion, important learning can emerge.

It's Good to Talk

There has been a great deal of study of the conflicting motivations that exist within relationships (or indeed within individuals them-selves), and a useful theory has been built up around the subject. This can provide a helpful device when it comes to analysing your own communication patterns. This way of understanding applies to any relationship – partners, friends and families. One or both people may be aware of tensions or they may not. A word of warning though: tensions are experienced in different ways by different people and the ideas presented below may not necessarily always reflect what happens in real life.

Communication theory is based on patterns between partners in a relationship as the result of opposing desires, values and needs. These opposing positions are set out below.

Conflicting Tensions

The underlying principles and sources of tensions revolve around:

- the desire to have close ties with others (connectedness) versus the need to be separate and unique (autonomy);
- the desire to divulge information (openness) versus the desire to be private (closedness);
- the desire for the relationship to be conventional (predictability) versus the desire for it to be original (novelty); and
- the desire for warmth to be genuine (affection) versus the desire for affection to be motivated by benefits and perceived advantages of the relationship (instrumental).

Thinking back to the case studies mentioned above, the conflicting tensions are clearly in action in all of them. There is evidence of one partner trying to control the relationship, lack of willingness to talk openly about what's going on and struggles for equality. Take a moment to consider if any of the issues mentioned here apply to your situation. It is worth examining your behaviour with another person as there can be issues affecting others that you may not be aware of. Giving feedback to each other on a regular basis can help avoid tension and arguments.

Arguments about trivial matters, or 'bickering' as Vera put it, may indicate some deep-seated issues or signs of other problems, such as isolation, loneliness or resentment. People may argue about mundane topics when their needs are not being met and/or when they are not communicating their needs to their partner. For relationships to be harmonious it's more effective when decisions are being made together and ideas and feelings shared.

You may wish to try some straightforward ways round some of these tensions, such as negotiating daily routines, giving your partner space, developing different interests, asking the other person about their views and feelings, having your own friends, and sharing together some activities, like holidays, or even trying some apart.

Most people are enthusiastic about the ideals of equality, openness and so on in relationships, but communication is not always straightforward. Understanding this can help us get our views across in a clear, honest and respectful way when talking together.

Talking Things Through

Relationships continue to change when people retire, sometimes more abruptly than anticipated, so they need regular attention. Tensions are common – indeed, they're to be expected – and don't go away. How people handle these tensions is what matters. It can make the difference between a well-adjusted and equal relationship in retirement or one that falls apart. There are conflict-resolution strategies and many sources of practical advice that suggest good communication can improve relationships, dissipate tension, and increase intimacy, trust and support (see the Resources section). The converse is true: poor communication can weaken relationships, exacerbate friction, create mistrust and even feelings of hate.

Lasting damage may result if you have unresolved conflict. The most useful advice is to tackle the underlying causes without delay. Another important point is that any existing problems in a relationship or friendship are likely to deteriorate. This is because when people retire they may be spending more time together, may not have the distractions of work or may be bored. It may come as a surprise when issues bubble to the surface suddenly and tensions become unbearable.

While people are working, it may be possible to ignore or avoid difficulties in relationships. Retirement often changes that. When partners spend more time alone together, hidden issues or resentments may emerge. But the good news is that retirement can provide the opportunity to resolve difficulties, and a few basic pointers about communicating may be a helpful reminder. Elizabeth Scott, a health educator, wellness coach and author, has put together some very helpful advice on improving relationships by using effective communication skills. We draw on her work here.

Developing effective communication	
Stay focused	Focus on your immediate feelings (not old grievances). Have understanding and a solution as your goals.
Listen carefully	Effective communication is a two-way process. Don't interrupt or get defensive. See their side, then explain yours.
Respond to criticism	Don't be defensive. Look for the accuracy in their view; that's valuable information. Admit when you're wrong or have made a mistake. It diffuses the situation.
Use 'I' statements	Make statements about your feelings, such as, 'I feel frustrated when ...'. It's less accusatory and helps the other person understand your position.
Look for compromise	Search for compromises to find a joint resolution, rather than trying to win. That's far more effective.
Take a break	If you feel yourself getting angry, take time to reflect.
Don't give up	If you both have a constructive attitude and mutual respect, conflict can be resolved.
Ask for help	If the situation is not improving, try other support or professional help.

You might want to use these ideas as a resource to approach dealing with tensions. While these strategies may be well known to you, it is possible to forget the most obvious ones in the heat of the moment.

Reducing Conflict

Clearly it's important for you to discuss changing situations with people who are closest to you. You need to consider the extent to which you want to be available to others, for example in a domestic role or in caring for grandchildren or in spending time with others. There may be family assumptions, especially about the care of grandchildren or of older or sick relatives. Traditionally women have been seen as the major carers, mainly unmarried women or women without children. You need to establish clear boundaries, particularly about the time you have available. When you first retire it may be difficult to be clear about your plans as there may be some ambivalence about what you want to do and how best to use your time. And during the years of your retirement your plans, priorities and passions may change.

One way of overcoming the 'Will you just …' assumptions is to trade tasks and skills, for example swapping the ironing of a shirt for doing some printing, rather like a bartering scheme. Looking after grandchildren or great-grandchildren may be enjoyable and satisfying if you want to do it, but it can become a burden rather than a pleasure. That's why it's so vital to continue to communicate your views about such responsibilities. The question of grandparents being paid for their time is a controversial one. A few require payment, some because they give up or forgo other paid work in order to undertake childcare. Some because they do not want to be taken for granted. Others who are more affluent wouldn't consider being paid. Situations or priorities may change – as people get older a caring role may become more exhausting. Anticipating complications means you can talk through them more easily when they occur. Raise issues as soon as you spot them.

New sources of conflict may emerge, around spending money, who cleans, who cooks, and so on. Regardless of the issue, it's important to identify what's happening. One partner or friend may not be aware of their insensitivity. Friendships may appear equal but it may be the case that one person dominates the conversation or is more demanding. Sometimes friendships may not work anymore, so it might be worth considering if you are in a friendship that either needs a radical overhaul or if it would be better to end it.

When Relationships Break Down

Life can present different challenges that retirees may not expect, such as not being able to find satisfactory purposes for the extra time. Sometimes you may be wondering what to do about your relationship if it is causing you problems. Or you may be concerned about your relationships with your children, which in turn are affecting your contact with your grandchildren. Or you may be lonely or depressed.

And sometimes it may be appropriate for you to seek professional help. It's a great idea to seek support from any professionally trained counsellor or coach – there is no shame in this as might have been considered in an earlier generation. Other strategies, including group and online support, are discussed elsewhere.

Many commentators in the media expressed surprise at the recent increase in the over-60s' divorce rate. The number of couples separating has increased by more than a third in a decade, as retirees are no longer content to remain in unhappy marriages. In 2010, a world record was set by two pensioners for being the oldest divorcing couple, both aged 98 – Bertie and Jessie Woods had been married 36 years. A total of 13,678 people over 60 were divorced in 2007, up from 12,636 the previous year, and up from 9,052 in 1997.

What is causing the rise in divorce in this age group? Divorce is often affordable for older people, especially when couples have paid off their mortgage and have sufficient equity. The increase in the number of people over 60 separating may be partly due to the more generous settlements being awarded than previously to women who have stayed at home to look after their family while their husbands concentrated on their careers. The landmark case of *White v White* in 2002 should be applauded. This case introduced a new touchstone of fairness when it was decided there should be no discrimination between the work involved in being a 'homemaker' and the financial contribution of the 'breadwinner'. As a result, an equal division of assets is becoming increasingly common. This takes into consideration the husband's pension. In these cases both partners may need to accept the idea of managing on just half the pension and scaling down expectations.

The so-called 'empty nest syndrome' may also play a role, with many couples getting divorced once their children leave home. This was the case for Theresa McGuigan. She was 62 when she and her husband decided to split up after 35 years of marriage. She said, 'We had such a good relationship in the early years of our marriage, especially when the children were at home. We had such fun. But when it was just the two of us things weren't fun anymore.' For Theresa there was no crunch point. They just slowly drifted apart.

In contrast, Peter Tuirney told us how shocked he was when his wife left him. He was 62, and had been married for almost 40 years.

> Like a lot of men I know, I had lived with my parents till I got married. I was just 23. When my wife Jean left me I did not realise how much I had relied on her. I was alone for the first time and was helpless. After a period of depression I decided to take control of my life. I began to get fit and lost two stones. It has turned out really well because I met someone and we are planning to marry. At first my two sons were a bit judgmental but now they accept my new partner and I feel closer to them.
>
> It is becoming evident that people aged 60 and over have much higher expectations of relationships than their parents did. They're looking forward to 20 or 30 more years of active and fulfilling life.

Important conclusions can be drawn from the 2009 statistics of *Saga* magazine that showed a 4 per cent increase in divorce figures for the over-60s:

- A huge social change has occurred. This generation is not behaving in the manner of previous generations.
- Some people in this age group are changing their identities. They seek to become more fulfilled by adopting a new image for themselves.
- Many challenge ageism and do not regard themselves as elderly. They achieve what they set out to do and are not defined by social mores.
- Many have high expectations, especially in their close relationships. With 20 or 30 more years to live they realise there is still time for new, more effective partnerships.

The awareness that life can change dramatically can be liberating for retirees, not just for those who are divorcing, and can provide opportunities for adventure and trying things they never had a chance earlier to do.

Life after divorce can certainly turn out well for some retirees. They are happy and looking forward to a new, fulfilling and exciting period. For others, however, particularly when one partner wanted to stay married, their new single status can seem bewildering and they can feel vulnerable and lonely.

Indeed, loneliness in general is a major issue for many older people, and for those individuals who have always appeared competent, the neglect by others, such as family or friends, may be casual, unintended and accidental. Loneliness is increasingly recognised as potentially damaging to an older person's health and well-being. The Campaign to End Loneliness was formed in order to support lonely individuals by offering them support from professionals and others who want to prevent such suffering (see the Resources section).

Despite being on their own, single retirees may still have to cope with many of the issues raised by the expectations of other people. Their family or friends may feel that without apparent ties the single retiree is available to undertake care of relatives or do favours. If you are living alone, you need to be clear about your own needs and desires and to discuss these issues with anyone who has expectations of you. This requirement is as great as it is for those in any partnership.

Most importantly, the single person may have relied more on work connections for their social life and their sense of worth. If this applies to you, you need to consider alternative ways in which this sense of belonging and meaningfulness can be achieved now that work connections have been left behind. This can be planned for to some extent by increasing social connectedness and taking part in activities such as volunteering.

Closing Thoughts

Life changes in retirement, sometimes in surprising ways. For partners, friends and family there may be many adjustments and compromises to make, such as in negotiating new routines and in sharing space. Resentment may be felt when one partner is still at work, under pressure, needing to meet deadlines, while the other one is having a ball – although there may be pangs of envy for both.

Friction may emerge when one person tries to control the relationship, when couples do not want to talk openly about what is going on, or when important decisions are made without consultation. Assumptions can lead to problems. New areas of tensions can emerge that may affect the whole family, as in the case of divorce.

It is worth repeating that, whether you are in a partnership or single, it's important that you establish clear boundaries – especially about the extent to which you want to be available to others, either in domestic or caring roles. Effective communication is key.

The good thing is that in retirement there is more time for you to interact with others, and as a consequence your relationships can become much more rewarding and fulfilling.

Chapter 8

Three Communities and More: Enriching Your Social Networks

It's a powerful idea that people need to belong to at least three communities in order to thrive. But why? Here are three good reasons:

- People need strong, stable relationships with others, relationships that are greater than simple acquaintances. Individuals need to give and receive affection and love from others.
- Humans have an inherent desire to belong and be an important part of something greater than themselves, whether it's family, friends, co-workers or a sports team.
- Loneliness is potentially damaging to an older person's health and well-being, so they need a certain minimum quantity of regular, satisfying, social interactions.

So you need intimate relationships over time – your family, partner, children or very close friends usually meet this need (your first community). You also need to belong to a larger group to feel you are part of something more important than yourself. When employed you often rely on your workplace (your second community) to meet this need. And you need sufficient social interactions to combat lone-liness and help you thrive – the third, and possibly fourth and fifth communities. Therefore, an important task in your retirement, when you have lost your work community, is to create new communities. Relying on your family and friends just isn't enough.

Fear and anxiety are often triggered at the thought of losing the work community, as people often rely on it on for status, compan-ionship and social interaction. That's hugely significant in your life. Margie, a woman in her 60s, who attended our retiring work-shops, said she came to understand her reluctance to retire when she considered how important her work community was in her life. She retired gradually from the organisation in which she worked for 32 years, which made the separation less acute. She cut her hours down over a five-year period from five days a week to one, before finally leaving. Then she continued to work occasionally as a consul-tant. Alex, a professor in our organisation, observed that leaving the secure community of work can be a 'tad scary': people can become overly attached to the institution of paid employment and the idea of labouring together. Many people worry about feeling lonely when they quit work, especially if they have only a small number of friends, live on their own or are not closely connected with their family.

This chapter looks at ways you can develop and maintain social networks outside the workplace, and why it is important to do so.

People's Reluctance to Leave the Work Community

Martin had worked as a lecturer, and he told us that when he was part of a large community, the university department, he enjoyed being greeted as he came to work. He loved working with colleagues, sharing ideas and jokes. He felt good knowing he was doing a good job and contributing to an important enterprise. Martin liked being asked for advice. To him that indicated he was making a differ-ence and was good at his job. He liked getting positive feedback from colleagues and students. When he was leaving, his colleagues expressed sadness as he would be missed. When Martin goes back now he is greeted like a long-lost friend.

To avoid the wrench of giving up the significant community of work, some people choose to keep some connection with their organisation. Creating special retirement communities for university staff is becoming a popular solution to this issue in the US. More than 60 such facilities exist there.

Physics World magazine discussed one example of a retirement community for physicists, which was set up in 1996 near Cornell University in Ithaca, New York. There are 340 residents in this community today, who either live independently or with assistance from nursing staff. Most of its members worked at Cornell at some point during their careers. Many still have offices and a bus runs from the site to the university every day. Other residents do voluntary work at the university, either at one of the local libraries or science museums. The intellectual atmosphere is vigorous, with more than 40 clubs and programmes having being created and managed by the residents themselves, including talks and lectures.

Some of the advantages of this community are that:

- the residents like the proximity to former colleagues and the opportunities to stay involved;
- it taps the knowledge and experience of older scientists and keeps them engaged;
- it helps to realise the goal of fostering strong community life; and
- it allows older scientists to continue to develop and contribute, even with the increasing care needs and limitations that ageing might impose.

As this workplace meets residents' needs well into older age, they are unlikely to leave. Such a confined life may not appeal to you. But it is clear why so many employees want to stay connected with their community: to satisfy their need to belong and increase their self-esteem. Retirees can continue to learn by maintaining links to their professional community. It's exciting to create and share new knowledge.

An example of continued connection to the workplace, but on a smaller scale, is through a *pro bono* scheme that includes retired staff. This has been a successful development in the university where we worked. The aim is to enhance the organisation's contribution to the wider community by providing professional experience, wisdom and knowledge to schools, including overseas. Retirees can play an important role in influencing events and practice, and it's also a good way for them to remain connected. They gain a sense of usefulness and kudos from belonging. It is worth checking out whether a similar connection is possible in your organisation.

Continued part-time work and less formal arrangements are also useful. Sally had worked in a lively organisation as a research officer and now she makes regular lunch engagements with former colleagues as a way of staying in touch. Others continue with their workplace friendships through regular contacts around shared interests, such as sport or visiting art galleries. There are many different ways that you can stay in touch, if that possibility appeals to you.

What's so Important about Community?

As we've mentioned, Martin felt bereft when he left his prestigious organisation. Now that he is connected to new communities, he's been able to analyse what it is he'd missed. He, like others, was interested in why his community was so important to him and what he needed to do in his life to replace them.

The word 'community' is derived from the Latin *communitas* (*cum*, 'with/together' and *munus*, 'gift'), a broad term for an organised society. The combination of being 'together' with 'gifts' is pleasing. A biological explanation suggests a community is a group of interacting organisms sharing an environment. For humans there's more to it than that. Shared aims or goals and beliefs, resources, needs and risks are necessary conditions that affect the identity of participants and the degree of cohesion. The environment can have a geographical boundary or – in the case of technologically advanced humans – a community can exist regardless of physical location.

In psychological terms a basic human need is to belong and be accepted, although this is more pronounced for some people and cultures. Human needs form a hierarchy – one level must be met before it is possible to move up to the next, according to American psychologist Abraham Maslow's famous theory of motivation.

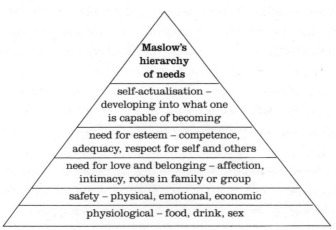

The need to belong has third place in this hierarchy after which esteem and self-actualisation can flourish. It's easy to see how retired staff members at Cornell University have all their needs met within their community; they belong, have respect, are expected to contribute ideas to the organisation and continue to learn.

But the need for *collective* human endeavour isn't explained in this hierarchy. In social psychology a 'sense of community' provides the key. The following two examples highlight important features that define our sense of community.

First, in talking about his choir, Malcolm told us that over the 10 years of its existence the 20 singers who are part of it have become very close; they care about each other, visit each other when one of them is unwell and have a special bond. They know that the group will put on really good concerts twice a year because of the level of commitment. They celebrate together and arrange outings to go to the opera and other musical productions a couple of times a year. He is proud of the success of this group and said it has made a huge difference to his retirement.

Second, Nicola, who is a retired librarian, talked to us about her support group, which was set up 12 years ago. She said how vital it is to her life and sense of well-being. She said she felt very happy to share her emotional problems with the rest of the group as all its members had developed such a strong sense of trust. As well as the regular monthly meetings, this group of 10 women have a special get-together about four times a year, and they all take food to share. They also arrange outings to the cinema and go on long walks in the summer where they take picnics. Their group is fun as well as having a serious function.

It is clear from the above examples that the group members matter to one another and their needs are met through their commitment to each other. They have clear boundaries, and as Nicola points out they have built emotional safety. The strong sense of belonging provides a sense of group identification. Another important feature is that each member has some influence in making decisions about what they are going to do and this provides a sense of cohesion. They all gain a sense of pleasure in their participation in the group and develop a shared emotional connection through joint endeavours, activities and experiences.

It is useful to reflect on these features to explain the importance of community in your life. When membership, influence and shared emotional connection are lost once you leave work, it is important to work out how these features can be replaced elsewhere.

The Workplace Community

In the workplace the elements of community have a dynamic interaction within and between each other. The workplace may allow people to use their influence, creating feelings of power, a sense of authority and some degree of control. People's influence can give them a sense of importance and a role in decision-making.

Being involved in a wider association is satisfying for two connected reasons. The success of the work carried out collectively may invoke a sense of pride, and this is especially the case if the values of the organisation are congruent with your own.

Shared emotional connection is the decisive element of a community. It includes shared history and shared participation. Therefore, having membership of a publicly recognised establishment, a modest or a prestigious one, can satisfy a sense of belonging. Leaving it can be disturbing. Margie, who we introduced earlier, spoke about how painful it was when, just as her retirement was announced, colleagues started to treat her as if she had already left. She felt ostracised by such insensitivity.

People's pride and sense of identity often come from a sense of belonging. For example, people often introduce themselves as working at a named organisation. With that comes prestige. People know who you are through your relationship with an organisation. Individuals may gain an identity through their workplace or role that in turn may bring emotional safety.

When Martin, who we talked about earlier, left his community he struggled for a long time when introducing himself – 'retired academic' was one title he tried, but that left him dissatisfied until he felt confident and bold enough to say: 'I'm a writer … a consultant …'. Developing new identities takes time. And Martin said that being a freelance or independent worker is hard at first without the strength and power of the work community for backing. He now enjoys both. He has developed confidence in his independent work, while also being attached to influential organisations as a consultant and coach on a part-time basis.

It's painful, even terrifying, to lose a sense of membership, influence and shared emotional connection – all at once. No wonder some retirees talk about the experience as being terribly overwhelming. The break can seem violent, brutal and rupturing. A major task for you is to find satisfying replacements. This may appear hard at first, so it is worth discussing with others. It might be that existing or former colleagues also feel the need to stay in touch. There may still be a role for you, if you want it, such as being a mentor or adviser. It's worth checking out.

Released into the Wild

It may take a while to adjust to a world without structure, security and predictability, says Alex Moore who was introduced earlier in the book. New networks are crucial for replacing your work community. The value of attending to them in advance is critical, as making new friends and feeling part of a new community are often a slow process. Preparation is key as Caroline explained. She replaced the community of work by building up and refreshing her other communities. This involved starting new activities with existing friends, embracing new friends and creating new social opportunities.

Think about the different types of communities, other than work or professional occupation, which may satisfy your need for a sense of belonging, esteem and security. These communities may be:

- family-based (relatives or chosen partners or friends);
- cultural (ethnic group; religion; particular need or identity – for example, retired people);
- geographical (local neighbourhood or street); and
- interest-based (leisure pursuits or specialist subjects).

Love, companionship, structure and a sense of belonging may be found in many of these groups. You may find that your membership is long-term or your involvement may be transient as your needs change over time.

Deepening Family Relationships

Retirees often want to spend more time with their loved ones. You may be looking forward to getting to know your family better.

Looking after grandchildren and/or older relatives and going on holiday as an extended family are seen to be very important for strengthening relationships and providing mutual support. Caroline points out that her grandchildren represent an extension of her most precious community.

Children and grandchildren need to have relationships with adults of all ages, many retirees argue. In Jennifer Evans's family, like so many others, there is a complicated network of stepchildren, half-brothers and sisters, aunts and uncles. She benefits from this extended family because so many live nearby and there are lots of places for her to go for support and encouragement. This family scenario is often different from that of previous generations. When Jennifer was bringing up her children there was very little support around. She says that leaving work has given many retirees the opportunity to be involved and useful – two very important antidotes to getting old and depressed.

Irene and John agree. They have an open house every Saturday for their three children and partners, their seven grandchildren and partners, and now their two great-grandchildren. They share a meal, an afternoon of catching up, fun and support.

Family life isn't always rosy. Some tensions in the family community may be felt as people get used to being at home together. Different tensions can emerge in any of these situations: having children, not having children, having grandchildren, being partnered, being single or living alone.

Despite the ageing population the number of multi-generational homes is rapidly declining, although the number of grandparents providing childcare for grandchildren is increasing. According to UK National Statistics, in 2008 in Great Britain:

- 30 per cent of women aged 65–74 lived alone compared with 20 per cent of men in this age group; and
- for those over 75 this figure increased to 63 per cent and 35 per cent respectively.

Without a strong family network people can experience a sense of disconnection from society, which may result in loneliness. Other social networks are required.

How to Develop and
Maintain Social Networks

Virtual Communities

'It can be a lifeline for people,' said Faye Williams, 74, of her local project to encourage older people to use the internet, claiming that it can be of special benefit to those who live in rural areas, have some disability or are lonely. More older people are active online now than in the past. When current retirees' parents retired 25 or 30 years ago, they had no experience of computers and of being involved in social networking. The virtual community is both a benefit and a challenge. The internet helps make and maintain vital relationships. Gill Adams of Digital Unite, a provider of online digital learning resources, explains:

> One Digital Unite project, which organises Silver Surfers' Day, is 'Schools for Silver Surfers' where a team of youngsters links up with local sheltered housing schemes to 'tutor' their elders. This has benefits for young and old alike, and helps make society a safer, more cohesive place – simply because age groups that often 'miss' each other, start to appreciate each other.

John Carbis, a retired Royal Engineer, suggests that more older people would go online if they had the right support, especially if courses were designed and run by older people. He says this would help get over the natural reaction of suspicion: 'Anything new is treated with a modicum of suspicion, which creates a barrier.' John now supervises the cybercafe at the Royal Hospital in Chelsea and offers courses to more than 60 regulars. As one satisfied Chelsea Pensioner explained:

We didn't know how to use a computer before – it was all totally new to us. Now I enjoy using the internet to look up my family tree and keep in touch with relatives all over the world ... Being given a free computer was marvellous – it's opened up a whole new world for us.

New groups like 'totally4women' are springing up (see the Resources section). This one claims to be a dynamic community for older women who are all about sharing their life experiences, passions and interests:

Now, we are winding up not winding down. We are setting up new businesses, changing our relationships, travelling, studying, doing sport (some of us!), volunteering ... and just getting on with life, with, above all, a desire to have fun and make each other laugh.

The term 'virtual community' is attributed to American author Howard Rheingold. He identified its potential benefits for psychological well-being, as well as for society. The virtual community describes a social network of individuals who interact through specific media, potentially crossing geographical, age, class, gender, ethnicity and political boundaries in order to pursue mutual interests or goals. The most pervasive is the online community. This community may not have such a strong bonding function as other face-to-face communities have, as there is less socialising, but it does have great value – particularly for older people who may have mobility issues. Recent studies have looked into the development of health-related communities that allow for conversations between people going through similar experiences. This is a means for people to develop a better understanding and behaviour towards their treatments and health practices.

Facebook, Twitter and blogging allow people to keep up to date with their friends without too much effort. Here, Anne Freeman describes how she stays in touch with her daughter who moved to Canada:

> I did a course on Photoshop in the first term (of my retirement) that has led to my spending lots of time working on my photographs and putting them on the internet site Flickr for others to share. I have [been taking] photos of the sunset from the bottom of my garden since January and am going to complete a whole year of this with a view to making a montage of the photos ... This has meant that my daughter in Vancouver can keep in touch with how the garden is progressing.

The benefits of the virtual community in satisfying older people's basic needs are now well established. The UK government encourages participation in virtual communities: in 2011, for example, it launched the Get Digital campaign aimed at older people in sheltered accommodation. This initiative included digital mentors helping older people develop the skills and confidence to use the internet safely and effectively. Age UK branches all over the country are also supporting older people with individual and group tuition, and older volunteers are offering their services as mentors. Having a person sitting next to you seems to be an important factor, especially if this person is older too.

Professional benefits can also increase. LinkedIn is a useful social networking site for professionals looking to find freelance work, exchange information, ideas and opportunities, and stay informed about their contacts and industry.

Searching for New Communities

In retirement you have opportunities both to extend existing social relationships and create new ones. Great satisfaction can be experienced from these. Some retirees set up new communities and networks before leaving work. You may find that being at home and alone more often means you need to pay more attention to seeing people on a regular basis.

Shared interests are frequently the basis of social networks, and retirees often join local groups. As Eileen suggests:

> My networks are hugely important. Making regular commitments to groups of people demonstrates how one values them. Belonging and engaging in them is important for one's self-esteem ... I belong to a sewing group that meets monthly, I meet friends for meals regularly, arrange special outings to the ballet ... My *a cappella* singing group meet weekly. We have a great laugh and produce great sound ranging from jazz to classical pieces. I can't think of anything else that provides such joy and sense of well-being.

Reading groups are very popular with retirees and various groups may exist locally (e.g., groups focusing on music, chess, bridge, conservation, rambling, fitness and sports, golf, political activism). You could join a single-age or mixed-age group. You will find the local council's website a good place to start searching, and libraries also provide good information.

For those who can't find what they want, starting a group with like-minded people is a great idea, but groups may not be as easy to maintain as imagined. Social groups may not have all the elements of a community and may not fulfil as many needs. They may take a long time to develop. In new groups there may be tensions when people exploit their influence or take over against the wishes of other members. This may create power struggles, especially in times of decision-making. And there are many decisions to make – about how often to meet, where to meet (e.g., in a neutral context or in people's homes), how the time is organised, what the purpose of the group is, how to include new members ... Starting a group requires much preparation about how different needs might be met; for example, the balance between socialising and its main function. All these issues will affect the group's cohesion.

Discovering the Local Community

Your local community can provide another important social network. Take Joanna's case, for example. Most of her career as a fitness instructor involved a daily commute that left little time for her to be involved locally. Now retired, she volunteers as a school grandparent governor. She loves her work as a volunteer, two afternoons a week in her local Citizens Advice Bureau and reading to children in her local primary school twice a week.

Councils provide many activities and events for locals of all ages, including older citizens. These aim to encourage the community to be more independent, raise general awareness about the environment and local services, and increase knowledge on social issues, health choices and so on. Retirees may also feel part of a community through their involvement in health and fitness activities (e.g., sport, visiting the gym regularly, yoga, Pilates). There are many local schemes for those interested in nature conservation, while others find a new sense of community through sharing an allotment.

If you used to travel to work you may not know your local area very well, nor have had much opportunity to become involved locally. 'I was amazed by what was around the corner,' Sophie told us:

> I joined my local library which is wonderful. The staff members are really helpful. I found a cafe in the same street and I often pop in and I'm getting to know the regulars. What's great is that people from all walks of life use it and I'm getting to know them. I've found a great stationery shop for my printing ink, a picture framers and a fab yarn shop. I'm doing a knitting class for beginners there. It's great fun and I'm mixing with a very different group of people.

Being retired means having the opportunity to use local resources and to make a contribution. People find new social contacts through volunteering activities. Martha, who gave up her career in banking, said:

I didn't expect to get so involved. I started as a counsellor at my local drop-in centre and I met a couple of wonderful women who also volunteer. I now see them socially. I was asked to become a trustee. It's been fantastic as I'm using my skills as both counsellor and accountant and this has boosted my confidence. I realise I still have a lot to offer.

The local community can make an important contribution to your new lifestyle, sense of identity and usefulness.

Going Further Afield and Settling in New Communities

Going to live by the sea, the countryside, the centre of town from the suburbs or abroad are some people's dreams. There are practical reasons too – to be near family, friends or healthcare facilities, or for easier transportation. Some relocate to live on cruise ships where they are looked after in a travelling hotel and get to see splendid countries and exotic sights around the world. What all these people have in common is that they are living in new communities. That can present challenges as well as enjoyment.

Retirement villages are growing in popularity. This concept differs from the professional retirement community discussed earlier as age alone unites those who live there. What attracts people to such a way of life? An extract from the Retirement Villages promotional website offers some evidence of what is on offer:

Wouldn't it be nice to live free of the stresses of modern life? To be surrounded by like-minded neighbours who want to get the most out of life? A safe community filled with social opportunities and beautifully landscaped outdoor spaces in which to retreat? ... That's exactly what [we] have to offer.

... Over the last ten years, Richmond Villages has created a number of highly successful Retirement Communities around the country with more in the pipeline. Our purpose-built villages are a new concept in retirement. They go further to meet the expectations and aspirations of retired people than ever before by offering a socially active and independent lifestyle, coupled with the reassurance of as much or as little care as they might ever need.

This retirement community offers a stress-free retreat, safety and reassurance, like-minded neighbours and social opportunities in pleasant surroundings. Reading between the lines it would appear that this publicity draws on older people's fears, offering firm boundaries between older people and the rest of society, especially other generations and cultures. This often results in a mono-cultural community, although what it lacks in diversity and richness it makes up for in safety and security.

But do all villages live up to their promises? A rather disturbing headline in the *Guardian* Society section on 22 May 2013 suggests not: 'Older people up in arms … Four years with no warden, no club, no security – it's hardly the stress-free retirement residents were led to expect.' Despite publicity that claimed the key benefits at one such retirement community would be the level of services provided and total peace of mind it afforded, residents reported that they didn't get the facilities promised. The lesson is clear: check everything out in advance.

Estate agents now provide crime statistics for people looking to move to specific areas. Crime mapping has advantages and drawbacks. It can reassure older people that crime isn't as bad as perceived. Publishing this information is a useful step in encouraging better community engagement to tackle neighbourhood issues. But the way the statistics are presented can be misleading and can increase the fear of crime. Playing on people's fears is highly suspect morally. While statistics show older people are less likely to become victims of crime than other groups, their fear of crime is shown to be significantly higher than other people's.

You might see a retirement village as an attractive halfway house between living independently and receiving nursing care. Some provide both facilities so that people can move in when they are in good health and then continue to live there when they need more support. Over 25,000 schemes exist across the UK. Most have a minimum age for residents (55 or 60), but the average age of someone moving in is 72, according to *Which?*. The advantages and disadvantages were spelt out by *Choice* magazine in July 2010.

Advantages	Disadvantages
Security and peace of mind	Small properties
No maintenance worries	Communal garden
Convenient location	Service charges
Special design for older people	Living exclusively with older people
Social life and companionship	Sticking to rules

It can be a benefit or a disadvantage to be part of a specific community for older people, depending on your outlook, *Choice* suggests. Living so close to neighbours, not mixing with younger people and feeling pressure to join in may be unappealing to you. But this way of living does have huge advantages. Having people around and feeling part of a lively community can bring joy to life. As an alternative to a specially constructed, and perhaps restricting retirement community, Jo Evans set up Rotherfield St Martin in East Sussex. This is a church-in-community charity. It is dedicated to providing a range of support services that enable village pensioners to remain in their own homes and maintain their cherished independence for as long as possible. It is based on the tradition of self-help and has become a vibrant club with over 300 members and 140 volunteers. *Saga* magazine, which published reports about such schemes in September 2012, asked readers to express an interest. Hundreds responded and attended a planning seminar. It could be a template for future care in the UK, *Saga* suggested.

In contrast to moving into a ready-made retirement village, a number of active retirees take enormous risks and leave the safety of their familiar surroundings to move abroad. While this often fulfils a lifelong dream, it is also a huge step and should not be undertaken lightly. The fictional retirees featured in *The Best Exotic Marigold Hotel* went to India looking for luxury and pampering in their retirement but did not find that – though they did find excitement and challenges that forced them to look at their lives in a new way. But these kinds of challenges can bring real problems for an adventurous retiree such as Allie, who went to live in France. She reveals some of the difficulties she encountered:

> It is not possible to be able to speak French immediately or be accepted into the local French community just like that. I have to work at it and it takes time. I have decided to try to find some voluntary work so that I will be interacting with French people and this should make me use the language more … My experiences here have made [me] understand some of the difficulties of being an 'immigrant' … My relationship with other English people here is tricky – on the one hand I need the useful knowledge and support they can give – on the other I am alarmed by how easy it is to speak English and mix only with other English people most of the time. I struggle to have a more authentic experience and hope I will succeed in making friends with French people who share my left-wing and feminist values.

As Allie discovered, life in a new country can be very rich but also very hard. There's a lot to learn about living in a new community, from how local democracy and village affairs work to the customs, culture and health system.

There are no rules for retirees in moving abroad, but if you are contemplating such an adventure there are some factors worth attending to. For example, it may be useful to rent a place before buying so you can live in the community prior to making a long-term commitment. It's also useful to check out the prospects for finances, health resources, social life and opportunities for a good social life. Moving abroad can be an adventure, and it can be hard work, especially if you live on your own or don't want to rely on the local expatriate community. Be warned though, in times of economic uncertainty the implications of currency exchange rates are massive. *Choice* magazine reported in July 2010 that the overseas retirement dream has turned sour because of low investment returns, hikes in the cost of healthcare, and the pound remaining consistently weak against both the euro and the dollar. This may mean a drop in your pension income. Learning a new language may be another challenge to consider. And if you move back home after a while it means restarting new communities and social networks. As in other matters, though, it is worth remembering that a decision to move abroad is rarely irrevocable.

Closing Thoughts

Once you have made the move from work to retirement your life may be rich in community involvement. You may experience a strong sense of community – membership, influence, integration and shared emotional connection – in a number of different groups. You may want to join forces for action (campaigning, political or voluntary work), take pleasure in getting to know your family and friends at a deeper level, and enjoy new groups of people who share your passions. Take note from other retirees who say it's important to belong to communities, so that you can build self-esteem and avoid depression. Some even think life wouldn't be worth living without membership in such social networks.

The need to belong, to feel secure, to sense continuity from one generation to another, to interact confidently and to make a contribution to different communities are all rated highly by retirees. Whereas geographical boundaries once dictated social network membership, in the new world of retirement older people are excited by the possibilities of the internet to extend their communities. Older people have many different needs and the types of communities that meet those needs vary enormously.

Your ideals of retirement communities will be your own versions, not other people's. They will feature aspects that are of value to you, such as people to share good food and laughter, fun and companionship, exchanging information, intellectual stimulation, learning challenges, excitement and tranquillity, security and safety, multi-generational interaction, multicultural richness, supporting others' learning and opportunities to share your wisdom. Enjoy.

Chapter 9

Is Retirement Good for Your Health?

This is a serious question: does retirement enhance your physical, mental and social well-being?

To address this question we consider the relationship between retirement and health, and how you can take charge of your own well-being. We also highlight the increasing importance of political and economic issues for a healthy ageing society.

Health consistently tops the list of what determines retirement satisfaction, even above financial security, retirement planning, participation in activities and marital status. People frequently say improvement in their health is a key goal in retirement. So the question deserves serious consideration.

The Relationship between Retirement, Health and Longevity

Is retirement good for your health? The answer isn't straightforward. Some research is reported in unhelpful ways. The question of whether your retirement will be good for your health depends on some complex issues and interconnected factors. Some of these are in your hands (e.g., your plans to enhance your health and well-being, your own resources to deal with stress), but other factors include the availability of local resources to support you.

There is much that can be gleaned from studying groups of workers around the world and what happens when they stop working. But you need to treat the results with caution, as reports investigating the health effects of retirement have been inconsistent – some suggest a beneficial effect and others conclude the reverse. Most importantly, researchers admit that explanations for research results are not always fully understood. But one message is clear. It is not retirement in itself that leads to depression or loss of good health. It is the need to substitute the good things that are lost when you stop working that might affect your health.

Startling news – people who retired at 55 had almost twice the risk of death compared with people who retired at 60, one study in 2009 on healthy ageing and longevity concluded. Well no, not so alarming – the explanation could be that people who retired at 55 chose to go early because of their declining health. This is an example of misleading news – what statistics suggest but cannot be explained. When people are in good health when they retire at 55 they are no more at risk. People who retired at 60 were no different than people who retired at 65, in terms of overall risk of death, the same study reported.

Reassuring news – retirement at age 60 had no effects on physical health functioning and, if anything, was associated with an improvement in mental health, particularly among those in higher employment grades. This was the conclusion of research with British civil servants in 2003. It was found that mental health functioning deteriorated among those who continued to work, but improved among the retired. And, not surprisingly, physical functioning declined in both working and retired civil servants.

Contradictory news – retiring does have a negative impact on health. Another study looked at 16,827 men in Greece in 2008 who had not been diagnosed with a health condition, such as diabetes, stroke, cancer or heart disease. It compared men who retired to those who were still working. It found that retirees had a 51 per cent increase in their risk of death (after controlling for things like wealth, education, marital status, and so on). Most of the increase in death risk was linked to heart disease and cardiovascular health.

Good news – retirement leads to a substantial reduction in mental and physical fatigue and depressive symptoms, and retirement does not change the risk of major chronic illnesses such as respiratory disease, diabetes and heart disease. There are a number of explanations for this finding according to the French researchers reporting in the *British Medical Journal*:

> If work is tiring for many older workers, the decrease in fatigue could simply reflect removal of the source of the problem … furthermore, retirement may allow people more time to engage in stimulating and restorative activities, such as physical exercise.

It's too early to make definite claims about positive and negative benefits from retirement at a particular age, these researchers suggest.

Some are cynical about such reports. In response to the headline 'Research says retirement is not good for us', Jenni Murray, presenter of *Woman's Hour* on BBC Radio 4, joked (in the *Observer* on 18 May 2013): 'Oh good grief … it's a conspiracy!'

> How clever of a government that's so strapped for cash to find a way of sweetening the pill of an ever-rising retirement age. Sorry, we can't afford to pay you to ease up in old age, but here's the good news: retirement is the first step towards one foot in the grave.

This report to which Jenni Murray was responding, published by the Institute of Economic Affairs and the Age Endeavour Fellowship, suggests that health improves for a short while immediately after retirement but then deteriorates quite quickly. It claims that clinical depression is 60 per cent more common in established (veteran) retirees and they are 40 per cent less likely to describe themselves as in good or excellent health than their working contemporaries.

But despite the contradictory evidence of the reports, most would agree that your own attitude to health is far more important than your retirement age. You do – to a large degree – hold the key to your health in your own hands. 'I've got it sussed,' claims Colin, a veteran retiree, when talking about staying healthy and avoiding depression. Four years ago, aged 69, he retired from working as a chauffeur when his boss moved to Spain. He explained:

> You've got to fill your time. I go to the gym Monday, Wednesday and Friday mornings for about an hour and a half. And sometimes on Saturday as well if I am not working. I drive an old guy in his 80s to golf and act as his caddy. That means a three-hour walk. I also drive my old boss when he comes back to visit his family. It's good to feel useful. The other days I use my bus pass and go to places like Sevenoaks and have a long walk. The gym exercises help keep my legs strong. Also going to the gym stops me eating. That's the one thing I have to be disciplined about. I never smoked or drank because of my job, which is good. And being more active means that I'm sleeping better. I don't need to get up really early and I don't rush around. That's what I like. When I worked full-time I was always rushing round and feeling stressed. I'm much more relaxed now.
>
> I hope the powers that be know what a godsend the bus pass is. I meet lots of people who are doing the same as me. We talk on our journeys and I talk to the younger lads in the gym. You've got to keep your brain active.

The message from Colin is clear. It is not retirement but the need to substitute the good things that are lost from not working that might affect health. To do this, Colin:

- has a clear purpose in his life;
- structures his days;
- makes a bit of extra money;

- feels useful;
- maintains social contact with colleagues and friends; and
- keeps his brain active.

And he exploits his new-found freedom and time to create opportunities for activities, keeping fit and exploring new places.

With some forethought and planning you can create a new purpose or purposes in retirement, earn a bit of extra money if required or make adjustments to your outgoings. You can make a contribution in new ways, such as volunteering, develop friendships and new communities, and use your time to keep healthy. Life can be rich in retirement and therefore the causes for depression and deterioration in health can be avoided.

Yes, there may be some ambiguity in the research findings, but nevertheless they contain important implications for government, policymakers and individuals.

First, government and policymakers need to reconsider health policies and health education to support the healthy lifestyles and health choices of older people, in all socio-economic groups, so the incidence of heart disease, stroke, diabetes and cancer can be reduced.

Second, as people will be working for longer and retiring later in life, efforts are needed to improve and adapt working conditions and employment policies. These measures will help older workers maintain good health.

Third, it's never too late for you to take action to enhance your health and well-being. So take encouragement from this.

What it Means to Be Healthy in Retirement – What Helps, What Hinders

Despite or because of retirement, many people are enjoying longer, healthier lives in our society. Expectations of staying healthy and living longer are much higher than before. Not all of us can reach 100, but increasing numbers of us do so, and some live even longer.

One such supercentenarian was Grace Adelaide Jones (7 December 1899 – 14 November 2013) of Bermondsey, London. At the age of 113 years, 342 days, she was the oldest verified living person in the UK, and the sixth-oldest person in the world until her death. Grace never married, but was engaged before her fiancé was killed during the First World War. She later turned down marriage proposals to look after her mother and siblings. She attributed her longevity to good food.

The current population of 10,000 centenarians in the UK could increase by more than 100-fold in the next 68 years, according to the government's population projection study. However, this masks huge variations between social groups (discussed later), and has serious implications for health resources. Living to a great age may not appeal to everyone if they are not enjoying an active and decent quality of life.

What Is Known about Maintaining Good Health?

Perceptions of what it is to be healthy are expanding. The World Health Organisation's definition suggests that health is not simply an absence of disease or infirmity – it is a state of complete physical, mental and social well-being, all of which are inextricably linked.

Knowledge about health and well-being is increasing and becoming more accessible via the internet. It is possible to access support either individually or through groups that help to manage health issues. The majority of retirees are very conscious of good physical health advice, as summarised in the table below. This information is what's generally recommended, just to serve as a reminder. All the 'shoulds', 'oughts', 'dos' and 'don'ts' have been removed to avoid the language of instruction and censure.

The unpalatable truth is that there's a strong connection between diet and the incidence of heart disease, stroke, diabetes and cancer (see the Resources section) – food intake and eating habits matter enormously. It's not just the non-existence of retirement that keeps people healthy in the remote communities we described in the introduction. People there don't have processed foods, take-aways, fizzy drinks or fast food. Their diets are full of natural and unprocessed foodstuff just like that recommended by 113-year-old Grace Adelaide Jones.

Physical health advice in a nutshell	
Eating	Aim to eat around five servings of fruit and vegetables daily and lots of fibre. Foods with high levels of trans-fat and processed foods, sugar, confectionery and salt need to be reduced. Dietary supplements, such as vitamins and minerals, aren't necessary if a balanced diet is eaten, unless recommended by your GP or dietician.
Drinking	The advice around alcohol is not straightforward ... a little of what you fancy does you good but the emphasis is on the little. The suggestion is to keep to around two units a day on average for women and three units a day on average for men, and to have days when no alcohol is consumed. Drink as much water as you can, but fizzy drinks often contain lots of sugar and chemicals so these are best avoided. Many sources suggest that increased fizzy drink consumption is a major factor contributing to osteoporosis.
Exercising	It's good to exercise daily but the type of exercise will depend on your present health status and interests. A variety of exercise is useful for retirees to maintain strength, flexibility, cardiovascular health and balance. So how much is enough? The NHS recommends at least 30 minutes of moderate exercise daily.
Smoking	Best not to.
Monitoring health	Regular health checks are effective as early detection of cancer and other diseases can prolong life.
Relaxing	Try not to transfer workday stress into retirement. Find ways of relaxing that suit you best.
Sleeping	The general consensus is that getting around seven or eight hours of sleep nightly will be beneficial. This may be difficult, especially if medication is taken, or if people have a disturbing condition, or if they are caring for others when sleep may be interrupted. It's suggested that prolonged sleep duration (daytime napping and over nine hours of night sleep) may be associated with an increased risk of dementia.

All good advice, but a short power nap may be OK. As the writer Gene Perret quipped: 'I enjoy waking up and not having to go to work. So I do it three or four times a day.'

Considering Our Well-Being

Being in good shape physically isn't the only key to health. 'Well-being' is a catch-all term that covers two further essential elements: feeling good and functioning well. Feelings of happiness, contentment, enjoyment, curiosity and engagement are characteristic of someone who has a positive life experience. Equally important is your functioning in the world. Experiencing positive relationships, having some control over your life and having a sense of purpose are all important attributes.

The growing belief that well-being is one of the more important aspects of our lives, both as individuals and as societies, is confirmed by the New Economics Foundation (NEF). The five ways to well-being that NEF recommends, which we have adapted below, have been incorporated into many local heath authorities' policies in the UK, as well as in other countries. The five ways to well-being chime with the key messages in this book, highlighting what's important in a good retirement.

The suggestions here are on a cheerier, more positive note, in line with feeling good and functioning well, and are often linked with happiness.

Five ways to well-being	Suggestions for achieving these
Connect	Connect with the people around you – family, friends, colleagues and neighbours, at home or in your local community. Think of these as the cornerstones of your life and invest time in developing them. It's been found that building these connections support and enrich life. It's important for retirees to feel part of at least three communities.

Be active	Walk or run, step outside, cycle, play, garden, dance. Most importantly, discover a physical activity you enjoy and that suits your level of mobility and fitness. It's been found that exercising makes people feel good.
Take notice	Be curious, catch sight of the beautiful, remark on the unusual, notice the changing seasons, relish the moment, whether you are walking, eating lunch or talking to friends. Be aware of the world around you and what you are feeling. It's been found that reflecting on experiences helps people appreciate what matters.
Keep learning	Try something new. Rediscover an old interest, try a course, take on a different responsibility, learn to play an instrument or how to cook your favourite food. Set a challenge that you will enjoy achieving. It's been found that learning new things makes people more confident as well as being fun.
Give	Do something nice for a friend or stranger, thank someone, smile, volunteer your time, join a community group, look out as well as in. It's been found that seeing yourself, and your happiness, linked to the wider community can be incredibly rewarding and creates connections with other people.

Three others are also important according to our research:

- Surprise yourself – be bold, be purposeful, adventurous, feel useful and fulfilled. Interests and passions may be rewarding, and activities such as volunteering provide social contact, contribute to society and develop new relationships.
- Have fun – take holidays, spend time doing new things, have new experiences and be stimulated.
- Act youthfully to stay youthful – seek occasions for fun, laughter and opportunities to experience wonder and awe, maintain a positive, ageless outlook and don't equate retirement with getting old and feeble.

A small improvement in well-being can help decrease some mental health problems, such as depression, and also help people to flourish.

Stress and Retirement

There can be a dark side. People talk about their fears and experiences of the stressful aspects of retirement. In coaching sessions, retiring workshops, and in social conversations, people speak of loss of identity and status, seeking a reason to get up in the morning, wanting to assert themselves as others make demands upon them, and so on. Stress is associated with the changes of retirement when a person's resources do not meet the demands of the situation. It can be confusing to be assailed by these stresses at the same time as feeling positive about the benefits of retiring. Such ambivalence is a disorienting experience.

Physical symptoms of stress indicate that something needs to be done. These symptoms include: interrupted sleep, headaches, inability to settle to tasks and loss of concentration. The Holmes and Rahe Stress Scale was developed to study the contribution of stress to illness. It's commonly used to measure stress by assigning points to events. Retirement is listed 10th, and scores 45 points. To put those 45 points in perspective, divorce scores 73, the death of a spouse 100, and a holiday scores 12. A score of 150–299 'means you have a moderate to high chance of becoming ill in the near future', and 300 or more indicates a very high risk.

Retirement affects many areas of your life. In looking at the possible stress burden of retirement (45 points), you might also need to factor in several of the following changes:

- financial state (38 points);
- different line of work (35 points);
- responsibilities at work (29 points);
- living conditions (25 points);
- personal habits (24 points);
- work hours or conditions (20 points);
- residence (20 points);
- recreation (19 points);
- social activities (18 points);
- eating habits (15 points); and
- holiday (12 points).

Altogether, if you have experienced change in all these areas since you retired, that's a whopping total of 300 stress points, reaching the high-risk zone. But don't be too alarmed. You need to consider three further ideas about stress in retiring.

First, stress results when 'demands exceed the personal and social resources the individual is able to mobilise'. In other words, your resources are a significant factor. Resources mean confidence and resilience, the experiences of change in the past, the ability to antici-pate problem areas and pleasures, and the available support.

Second, one reason people don't mobilise enough resources is that they do not realise that they need to, or do not know what resources are available to them.

Third, the score of 300 suggests retirement and the associated changes happen simultaneously, whereas, in many cases, the changes can be managed gradually. Fortunately the stress involved in retiring usually passes.

We can draw lessons: anticipate, marshal resources including asking for support, and move through the changes at the pace that suits your situation.

Activity may be the perfect antidote for periods of stress or anxiety, and a 'psychological first-aid kit' provides a valuable resource. This is the idea that psychologists Denise Johnson and Jill Chaplin recommend (see the Resources section). Their conclusion is that it may be obvious that certain activities, however modest, might make you feel better, but when you feel awful you can't always remember what they might be. Drawing them, using photographs, or even just writing a list, can serve as a useful cue to distract you and improve how you feel. The following activities have been found to improve people's mood. Some involve physical activity, some intellectual or creative involvement, and some are about being sociable. Try some:

- listening to music or playing a musical instrument;
- singing;
- reading a good book;
- drawing;

- making bread;
- watching a film;
- sport such as cycling, swimming or running;
- gardening;
- yoga or meditation;
- a glass of wine;
- game of darts in pub;
- a good meal; and
- a walk in the park or a beauty spot.

Other strategies also include expressive communication, like talking to someone or writing a letter. Denise told us:

> There is plenty of psychological evidence of the therapeutic benefits of such things as music or sport or socialisation but such things are individual. I have a psychological first aid kit and I still look at it sometimes and realise that there are more things that would make a positive difference to me. Often that's all it takes to initiate the first step towards an improvement in my mood …
>
> I certainly recommend it as a joint exercise. It's often surprising what people come out with when they think about it.

Denise and Jill found there was a clear split between those who needed human company if they felt low and those who wanted a more solitary experience. The point is to find activities that suit you best and to have a reservoir of ideas for what to do if you feel sad, stressed, anxious or dispirited.

Enhancing Our Health and Well-Being

One thing's certain: having knowledge about health and well-being doesn't automatically change your behaviour. It can be a lifelong challenge to maintain physical, mental and social well-being, and there is a danger of blaming people with poor health for their lifestyle choices. That's why this chapter ends by considering why health and well-being are more than an individual responsibility.

You may have 20 to 30 or more years of retired life. While many look forward to a more restful time, others embrace new occupations. A recipe for a good day includes: some exercise, a good laugh and achieving something.

Enhancing your health has a knock-on effect. For example, engaging in exercise and connecting with others in a social capacity will have a positive effect on your mental outlook. Retirement can mean having more time to attend to health and well-being – for example, in the choice of foods and where to buy less expensive fresh ingredients. Others pay more attention to exercise. Some do both.

So how do people fit exercise into their lives? Four trends emerge.

Exercise trends	
A regular, structured approach	Ruby visits the gym three times a week for two-and-a-half hours each visit. She fits this round her freelance work in the jewellery trade. John and Henri work out together having met at a clinic for people with heart problems. Swimming, Jennifer claims, is the ideal exercise for those between 60 and 70 and she goes regularly with her grandchildren. There has been a huge take-up in Pilates, yoga and golf, which need regular scheduling.
Exercising as part of a daily routine	Alan and Jean walk their dogs every day in the park and meet up with other dog walkers, and sit and chat while the dogs chase each other! Clive gave up his car when he left work and now cycles everywhere. Alice told us that she likes to keep active doing her housework, cooking, cleaning and shopping every day. She walks to and from bingo. For fun she sings in her local club in south London.
Incorporating exercise within a social setting	Kathy, aged 101, goes to ballroom dancing three times a week and away on dancing weekends with her partner David. A group of four retirees meet each week at a leisure centre and take part in morning exercise classes such as Tums and Bums, Gentle Exercise and Aqua-Aerobics before having lunch together.
Being spontaneous	Mike goes for long walks with his grandchildren whenever they pop round and has walking holidays a couple of times a year. Sophie runs round the block after she needs a break from writing her new cookery book.

Whatever type of exercise routine you choose, the advice is to keep it frequent and regular. Some retirees use a pedometer to count their steps. The NHS recommends at least 10,000 a day. This is also a good reason to get out of the house every day. Some local authorities and rambling groups organise guided walks for people who find it dull to walk alone.

Age is no barrier to exercise, as the following stories confirm. When Doris Long was 95, she set a new world record as the world's oldest abseiler by descending 70ft (21m) down a Portsmouth office block. When asked if she would do it again she said: 'This time next year I hope, and until I'm 100, then I'll retire.' The latest is that at 99 Doris is still abseiling. She told the *Sun*: 'It was exhilarating, I'm having an exciting old age.' This time she descended 328ft (100m) at the Spinnaker Tower, Portsmouth. Reaching higher is a Japanese man, Yuichiro Miura, aged 80, the oldest man to climb Everest. He claimed that 'this is the world's best feeling', adding: 'Although totally exhausted, even at 80 I can still do quite well.' Indeed! Tamae Watanabe, also Japanese, is the oldest woman to scale the world's highest mountain, aged 73.

However, retiring successfully and ageing actively are much-contested concepts in social gerontology (the study of ageing). Very active lifestyles do not suit everybody. Some people cannot or don't want to be active. Choosing more sedentary occupations is important too.

Increasing social connectedness is crucial for your well-being, health and happiness. As you age, your social circle shrinks, due to retirement and the deaths of friends and relatives. But, despite social stereotypes depicting older people as isolated and lonely, some actually connect with others more than younger people. People in their 80s are twice as likely to socialise with neighbours, engage in religious activities, volunteer in the community and attend weekly meetings of organised groups than those in their 50s and 60s. This isn't surprising as most people in the younger age groups will be at work and relying on colleagues for their social interactions.

Volunteering, another way to increase social contact, is also more prevalent among older people as retirees have more time at their disposal. Statistics confirm this: nearly a quarter of those in their 70s and 80s volunteer weekly, compared with less than a fifth of those in their late 50s. People who volunteer report better health and greater happiness than people who don't.

The Increasing Importance of Political and Economic Issues for a Healthy, Ageing Society

Is retirement good for your health? Well it may depend on where you live, your income, your level of education and your sex. Your healthiness and longevity are partly determined by factors beyond your control. This society is unequal and ageist and has a strong culpability culture. That is why it is important to stress that there's a danger of blaming those with poor health for their lifestyle choices.

Since our mothers' days there's been a huge shift in the ways fitness and health are viewed, and there's now considerable pressure placed on individuals to stay fit. The government uses various tactics, including 'nudging', a concept introduced by American writers Cass Sunstein and Richard Thaler, to persuade us to stay healthy, partly for economic reasons. They suggest it is possible to design environments that make it more likely for us to act in our own interests and demonstrate how 'choice architecture' can be established to gently propel – or nudge – us in beneficial directions without restricting choices available. In 2010, the Fabian Society reported that:

> With the direct costs of the ageing society rising to £300 billion by 2025 we need to get ahead of the challenge by changing people's lifestyles while they are still in their 50s and 60s. Research shows this could have a beneficial effect on later life.

The north–south health divide in the UK is well known. The divide is increasing and likely to worsen in the recession. Those living in the north are 20 per cent more likely to die before they reach 75 than those in the south, and a 2011 Manchester University and Manchester City Council report suggested that government policies have not reduced inequalities or regenerated local communities.

Wealth determines health. Far from the simple north–south divide, the starkest differences may occur between neighbours. Although the UK's average life expectancy is high (78 for men and 82 for women, according to the Office for National Statistics), this masks huge variation between social groups.

Wellington Archibold, 67, for example, lives and works as a cleaner in the royal borough of Kensington and Chelsea in London. The residents in St Charles ward where he lives can only expect to live to 73, whereas in the nearby ward of Courtfield, men can expect to live to 85. Wellington told the *Guardian* in February 2011 that despite being over the pension age he is still working a 45-hour week. He likes his work and it helps him pay the relatively high rent although he is putting his health at risk cleaning his estate throughout winter.

A vicious circle exists: poorer areas have inferior housing, fewer parks and transportation links; the statistics suggest that more people smoke and drink alcohol in these locations. People who live in poorer neighbourhoods are more likely to work in lower income jobs or are unemployed – there is a complex interaction of factors.

Inequality and ageism impact the health of older people, reports Age UK, and it calls on government to tackle pensioner poverty and promote healthy living in later life. It lobbies for local authorities to provide accessible and affordable leisure activities close to where older people live. Their health has been routinely overlooked, it claims, and inadequate income has a major impact on older people's health.

Education, not income or race, is the most important indicator of health during older age, conclude researchers at Princeton University. There is a link between additional years of education, longer life spans and better health during older age. But Richard Suzman, programme director of the National Institute on Aging in the US, said in his report on better health during older age: 'We have only a vague idea of when and where early experience links to old age or when and where to intervene.'

Higher levels of education have been linked to lower levels of heart disease in the UK (see the Resources section). Blood pressure could be the reason, researchers suggest: low educational attainment has been demonstrated to predispose individuals to high strain jobs, characterised by high levels of demand and low levels of control, which have been associated with raised blood pressure. Less educated women are more likely to experience depression, be single parents, be living in impoverished areas and below the poverty line.

Women live longer than men. In the past, explanations for this were about lifestyle and the labour-intensive work that men tended to do. But sports scientists at Liverpool John Moores University think they have a physiological explanation: women's hearts are stronger. Women's longevity may be linked to the way their hearts age – maintaining pumping power as they get older.

Important lessons about perceptions of retirement and older age or being 'elderly' in our society are challenged by the research findings from societies where the concept of retirement doesn't exist. People in these societies do not think of themselves as 'retired', 'old', 'worthless' or 'useless'. Younger people there do not have negative views of their 'elders'. But, in *our* ageist society older people are discriminated against on grounds of their chronological age. Ageism is deep rooted and widespread, and it influences many health policies and practices. This needs to be eradicated.

The message is to make your life more like those who live in cultures where the concept of retirement is unknown, including altering perceptions about the need to slow down at 65 and shifting the view that bodies and minds deteriorate earlier than they do. To do this you need to avoid some of the age-related attitudes so common in our society and challenge ageism, including ageist attitudes and language.

You may wonder to what extent attitudes will change following the abolition of the fixed retirement age. Views of retirement and of people older than 60 or 65 can change.

Closing Thoughts

It is worth reminding yourself that it is not retirement in itself that leads to depression or loss of good health. You need to find substitutes for the good things that you lose when you stop working. You need a sense of purpose, some control over your life, positive relationships, to be connected with the outside world, to be active, to eat well, to keep learning, to be generous with your time, to have fun and to act youthfully.

Health and well-being depend on many interrelated factors – physical, mental, social, economic, environmental and political. Some issues are beyond your control, but in retirement you have the opportunity to consider your health and make choices about what you can do to enhance your well-being.

There are many factors that affect your health, such as education and social class. Even the concept of retirement may influence your attitude to health, how you live your life and how you view yourself as you get older. There are many constructive steps you can take, so get moving, maintain a positive attitude, see friends and live as well as you can.

Chapter 10
The Spaces You Live in

Many retirees reacted with outrage at the suggestion that older people should downsize. Blatant ageism underpins the proposal to release large properties for those who 'really' need them. Using incentives to encourage retirees to downsize is insulting. While downsizing can be a great idea for those who are excited by its possibilities, putting moral pressure onto older people to move has angered many. Retirees' homes are more than accommodation with 'spare' rooms. They are a crucial link to neighbours and a community. Retirees' homes, spaces around them and a sense of security are key for well-being and need to be respected. We need to challenge the assumption that retirees need less space, will be less active, will want to move to the country or near the sea, will want to be close to other older people and be content with living in a restricted community.

You will probably spend more time at home during the day when you retire and that is likely to create the desire to use your spaces differently. How spaces are seen and used can be liberating. If it is the time for you to act, you will want to consider the options open to you. This chapter looks at the various possibilities.

Is Downsizing Good for Retirees?

Downsizing can be the perfect solution as Maureen discovered. She moved from inner city Birmingham to Bournemouth, having sold her hairdressing business.

> I didn't need a financial incentive to move to downsize. I felt lost in my large house once my children had left home so I bought a one-bedroom, ground floor flat. I like the fact that I can clean my flat myself rather than pay someone to do it. I don't need a gardener any more either as the communal space is the responsibility of the managers. I do like sitting outside when it's sunny. I couldn't bear to be cooped up. At first the space seemed rather cramped but gradually I adapted and the benefits far outweigh the disadvantages. There are no stairs to climb. I have no worries about the condition of the house, its maintenance or the cost of heating. My flat is easier and cheaper to run, and is much more manageable. Downsizing has released capital which I enjoy spending on lovely holidays. It has worked out well and I am very happy. People stay in local bed-and-breakfast places when they want to visit me so I don't have to get up early to make them breakfast and they have somewhere of their own to go to rather than feel they have to hang around in my place for longer than we both would like.

Maureen moved six years ago and is very happy with her decision. In her case there was no pressure on her. She hadn't felt guilty about living in her larger house. It was a judicious move that really suited her. Others want to downsize but don't want to live alone and see the advantages of sharing, not just because they get more space for their money but for the company and support of others. For example, June Green, Jenny Betts and Greta Wilson took the bold decision to set up house together and have reflected on their learning in a humorous, thought-provoking and practical book, *An Experiment in Living: Sharing a House in Later Life.*

Adam, who is a semi-retired architect, is angered by the assumption that he should downsize:

> Here we go again – blame the baby boomers. They say my home is too big for me. I should move to provide a home for younger people. What on earth do I need with a spare bedroom or two and a garden?
>
> Well, I love my house. I have lived in it for 40 years. I worked really hard to pay off the mortgage and feel I am being penalised for my thrift. I brought up my daughter here. My wife died here. The rooms are full of their things and everywhere I turn I am reminded of them. My daughter, her husband and their two boys and other friends come to stay. I am able to put them up over Christmas and other holidays as well. I use one of my so-called 'spare' rooms as an office as I work at home and I have a lodger to earn some money. I don't just live in my house. I live in my street, my neighbourhood, my community. I'm part of that and it stops me feeling isolated and lonely and I contribute to my community. There are loads of other ways to solve the housing crisis. Why focus on older people moving from their homes? This is such an ageist policy and the treatment of older people is disgusting. What next – an annual culling of the elderly?

Adam, like many retirees, is furious at the assumption that he should give up his home, move to a strange place and into a smaller dwelling to make way for younger people. Older people need to be seen as an asset, not a liability, argues the journalist and broadcaster Yvonne Roberts. Segregation in the 21st century is not a good idea, she wrote in the *Observer* on 23 October 2011. Neighbourhoods that thrive have a balanced mix, she says, 'not too many older people, not too many youngsters, not too many children. An exodus of older people would destabilise the balance.'

Guardian journalist Suzanne Moore moved into a smaller property to provide for her grown-up children, not to live on the profits from the sale of her home. She is far from being selfish (or flighty), as she plans to share the benefits of her good fortune with the next generation. On 23 May 2013 she wrote:

> The truth is that like anyone who bought property 20 years ago in London and tarted it up and just kind of lived in it, the profit made has nothing to do with my canniness or financial nous. It's just that house prices have soared. I am the beneficiary of that. My children are its victims ... When the haves – people like me – get worried not only about their own futures but those of their kids, the have-nots are really doomed ... It is *the* cross-generational, cross-class issue that we have to focus on. Still, like most things, this crisis is my fault as I read yesterday in a headline in *The Times* that said: 'Flighty older women to blame for pushing up house prices.'

Older people should not be pressured into feeling guilty about the housing problems of the next generation. Policy solutions could include building more houses or putting innovative ideas into practice (e.g., updating empty local authority houses, housing associations and private homes). If new homes were built, thousands of people would be employed too. This would have a positive impact on the economy.

People need to feel they belong, have a sense of well-being, and be of use to their wider family and community. Moving house may destroy all this. A home is also a link to neighbours and an anchor to the community. It is a store of memories – crucial to older people with dementia, a third of whom live in their own homes. Retirees report how difficult it is for their parents who have dementia to find their way around strange places. Staying in their own home avoids further confusion. It is also hard for wheelchair users to realise that they have to leave the home they love for accommodation on one level. Decisions around moving are often stressful. However, moving to alternative accommodation before it becomes too problematic is advisable.

Upsizing is also an option, especially when people move out of expensive city housing. Marion and John decided to move in together after being in a relationship for 10 years. They sold their individual properties and bought a large house together. The attraction was the hillside garden. This had been neglected for the last two years, as the previous owner could no longer care for it. Marion and John love working on the different parts of the garden – the raised vegetable beds, the tropical plant areas, the orchards – and enjoy the various sitting spaces where they relax and enjoy the views. Marion is in the process of converting the garage into an upholstery studio and John is restoring the three greenhouses. The house itself has a large conservatory in which they have monthly jamming sessions with local musicians.

This is exactly the sort of change some retirees crave, as they need more space for fun and activity rather than less. This is not the dominant image of retirees' lives portrayed in the media.

Serendipity sometimes plays a role. This was the case for Matt and Noreen who moved into a hotel while waiting for a new flat to be built. They had sold their big house and had money in the bank. They waited months for the builders to finish and in that time got used to a new way of living in their spacious room, with the lovely hotel swimming pool and spa, live Irish music twice a week and 24-hour room service. Neither cared to cook any more and they worked out that at £100 per night they could stay for as many years as they needed. They collected a few bits that were in storage and sold the rest. They love the idea of not being responsible for a property any more, and there are always interesting guests to talk to in the huge and very comfortable lounge. They are not the only ones to consider this option as we read in the *Guardian* on 7 January 2013:

One of the many irritants of ageing is how difficult it becomes to do even the simplest jobs around the house. At first it may only be stiff jam jars, but soon everything – from baths to cookers – gets to be a challenge … For moderately wealthy people, hotels can be very practical … At around £70 per night, for instance, it is cheaper for you and your lucky partner to live in a double room in a central London Travelodge than to rent many two-bedroom flats nearby. That includes bills, remember, plus all the breakfast you can face. The cheapest room at the Ritz, meanwhile, costs £285 per night – or a little over £8,500 per calendar month.

Retired people may end up moving more than once if they do upsize or downsize, with their next move possibly being to specialist accommodation (e.g., a retirement village or sheltered accommodation), and with potentially another relocation to a care home later.

Staying Put? Upsizing?
Downsizing? Going Abroad?
Moving to Specialist Accommodation?

No longer tied to an area near work, you can now think about your options. Some may like the idea of moving nearer to family or friends, or buying or renting some form of retirement accommodation. Decisions about moving require much thought and planning (see box). Since retirement may span several decades, a housing choice that seemed good for early retirement may be unsuitable later, which implies the need for another possible move in the future.

Staying or moving?

	Advantages	**Disadvantages**
Staying put	Opportunities to adapt your home to suit your needs (e.g., turning a bedroom into a studio, putting in a stair lift) Letting a room or converting the attic/garage into more useful space Adding an extension, conservatory or new kitchen	May no longer suit your needs, you may feel trapped and long for something new and more appropriate You may not have the energy or enthusiasm to make changes You may not be able to afford large bills or manage the garden
Upsizing	Having room for new interests and more space for possessions and collections Having more space for entertaining and having people to stay	Larger bills More difficult to manage as you get older May need to move again
Downsizing	Having manageable accommodation Smaller bills and may have extra cash Fewer responsibilities	Need to de-clutter and lose treasured possessions May feel claustrophobic Stress in selling and buying property
Going abroad	Exciting and challenging, fulfilling a dream New opportunities New networks and communities	Losing contact with friends Need to adjust to change in political climate and culture, or difficulties in learning a new language or paying for healthcare Drop in the purchasing power of your pension

	Advantages (cont.)	Disadvantages (cont.)
Moving to specialist accommodation	Security, resident caretaker Communal facilities, meals provided Care provision	Parting with possessions Difficulty in adapting May feel cut off from rest of community

Moving can be very stressful, so you need to consider your options carefully and get advice from your family and friends before making a big decision.

Barbara found herself needing to reassess her priorities. Since retiring from work as a teacher, much of her time during the first months was taken up with sorting out what to do with the house that she co-owned for 16 years and had to sell. Her feelings about moving turned out to be much more important than those triggered by retiring. She and others in similar situations find that when moving and retiring happen simultaneously there can be a much longer period of readjustment.

When Barbara downsized she used the Freecycle website to find new homes for her unwanted items (see the Resources section). She was pleased that so many of her pieces of furniture and other objects were of such value to other people in her community, and was most amused one day when a young man took her fridge away on his skateboard.

In considering a move to a new neighbourhood, whether at home or abroad, your future needs must be assessed. Good preparation means you should investigate the following in your chosen location:

1. Health resources – both physiological and psychological;
2. Social resources – family, friends, social networks;
3. Economic resources – income and savings;
4. Community and neighbourhood resources – local neighbourhood services and facilities, transport, community safety; and
5. Material resources – possessions, housing and transport.

The above research findings, listed in order of significance, show the resources that contribute to people's well-being after retirement (for more information see the Resources section).

Downsizing and De-Cluttering

'It sounds so simple, but in the past couple of weeks I have discovered that downsizing is, in fact, hideously difficult, like struggling into a smaller dress size or forcing your feet into a tiny glass slipper,' television presenter Esther Rantzen told the *Mail* on 30 March 2011. It seems that our possessions may be a joy to us or may become a burden. Our relationship with our possessions, not the possessions themselves, is the important factor here.

Jane Miller, author of *Crazy Age*, reflects on her life and thoughts on being old. She has an interesting perspective on 'clutter':

> And if I find myself clinging to objects and photographs, it is not so much because they remind me of the past or bring it back, but because I use them as aids or prompts in order to help me construct a private narrative I sometimes like to recite to myself about my own life, but also about the lives of people I once knew, who are now dead. Mementoes are there instead of memory, or to provoke memories … heaps of theatre and concert programmes and exhibition notes. I don't want them, and can't imagine why I've kept them. Is it in order to prove that I've done these things, seen them, been alive?

These reflections help us understand our relationship with stuff and how difficult downsizing and de-cluttering can be. The show *On Ageing* directed by David Harradine and Sam Butler also reveals our significant relationship with belongings. The show pieces together the memories of a selection of people (presented by seven children aged between seven and 13), and is sustained by two basic notions: that children live in the immediate present, while ageing is a process of the accumulation of memories and objects, the slow accumulation of years. This partly explains why moving home may be a traumatic event for older people, as in cases when they might move to specialised accommodation and must part with a great deal of their valued belongings. Conversely, downsizing provides the opportunity to get rid of unwanted clutter, items that have no value or attachment, which may be a process that is welcomed. And you don't have to move house to de-clutter. This can be a very liberating activity and as a result your home could become a much more enjoyable space in which to live.

Rethinking One's Accommodation

Being employed for many years may mean that your living accommodation has been neglected. Considering your home environment is an important task, as the percentage of time you spend in it will probably increase. Making the house and outside spaces work for you in retirement is a very useful job, ensuring that your environment supports you in living life to the full. Your home can have an important effect on your attitude and feelings towards retirement and ageing. Physical settings can affect your mood, memories, personal values and preferences towards the range and type of activities carried out there. Your home is more than a physical space. It is a place where you are surrounded by your possessions – an accumulation of memories and objects as Adam described earlier.

The most effective changes will be to create spaces that are more appropriate for your new lifestyle, allowing for new creative, recreational and social activities. Small changes can often create huge benefits, to reflect different and changing needs. The creative use of existing spaces or the addition of new spaces can have dramatic effects on your activities and life.

One significant change may occur when a couple are both retired and find they each need more space of their own (e.g., a study, work area or designated space) in order to pursue their own particular interests. It's worth repeating that many tensions arise in relationships when people start sharing a space for much longer than they used to. It's critical to discuss your needs, and the adjustments that you and others need to make, in order to live in harmony.

Some retirees start to sort out tasks that have been on their to-do list for a long time. 'Things I will put up with no longer' is a list of those niggling little annoying jobs – repairing the dishwasher, getting a damp patch on the wall sorted and so on. Once achieved, these tasks can bring a sense of relief and satisfaction.

Outside Spaces

The garden, for those who have one, might be a place where some sort of outbuilding (e.g., a shed, summer house, garden room, office) could be built. This provides an additional area, including storage space. For those wishing to work from home, an outbuilding can be useful when space inside is limited. The cost may not be that great, and a shed or garden room may add value to the property and may not require planning permission.

A shed, garden room, converted garage or summer house can be one of the most practical additions to a garden, and for retirees it has the potential to be a centre of creativity. As well as being useful as storage areas, such as for tools and garden furniture, they can also be used as a place to seek inspiration and work. The *Guardian* reports that a number of artists and writers, such as Damien Hirst, work in their garden sheds – a pleasurable working space that's quiet and peaceful.

Another retiree, Melanie Finch, took up painting in her garden studio after early retirement from teaching in Dorchester. Melanie now has the time to devote to her painting and loves featuring the Dorset coast in her work. Others have created garden spaces for pottery, stained glass and sewing.

The construction of the shed itself can provide pleasure. A recycling enthusiast, Tim Massey, told the *Knutsford Guardian* on 15 June 2010 that he built an eco-friendly garden shed with reclaimed timber and broken glass. The building, constructed from recycled materials, took nine months to build as it involved a lot of time searching for suitable resources. He said that the end result was worth it as he has built the perfect spot for him to relax.

Nature lovers can find a garden a wonderful haven for relaxing and birdwatching. Creating a pond can provide a fascinating environment for wildlife. In small gardens (or if you do not want the hard work of digging), free-standing ponds can be constructed easily and are available in many different sizes in garden centres. Building a pond is one of the most helpful actions anyone can take to help wildlife prosper (see the Resources section).

Making Money from Your Home

All the rooms in your house have important functions. Adam, who we talked about earlier, is still working part-time at home and uses one room as an office. He has a lodger to make additional money. Sixty-eight per cent of householders aged over 65 own their own homes outright. But a large percentage of those have extended their mortgages to give their children a lump sum and a chance to buy a home. Others are contemplating selling to meet nursing home fees or subsidise their grown-up children.

'Asset-rich and cash-poor' describes some retirees, says Annie Shaw in an article in *Choice* magazine. She states that they may be surrounded by things like a valuable house and garden, but may have little ready cash. The article, appropriately called 'Making Money without Lifting a Finger', recommends some ways of putting your assets to work:

- **Renting out a room in your house**
  Letting furnished rooms can earn you £4,250 a year tax free (£2,125 if letting jointly, but this figure may change) under the Rent-a-Room scheme. Caroline rents out one room and finds this very helpful in sharing the bills, but even so there are costs (e.g., extra light and heat, and maintenance). There may be a

higher home insurance premium too. As long as the income stays below the threshold there is no tax to pay. Anything above that figure needs to be taxed in the usual way.

- **Short lets**
  A short let may be suitable for overseas students. This is how Dorothea earns extra money and she provides breakfast and an evening meal as well, making £200 a week. Shamus rents out a room from Monday to Friday. He says the main advantage is that you have your home to yourself at the weekends. Insurance policies need to be checked and regular B&B providers could be liable for business rates.

- **Renting your drive**
  Maurice, who lives near Exeter airport, rents out his drive. Others who live near busy venues or stations find they have a waiting list. You can sign up to a matchmaking website. The payment you can get varies enormously. But remember: legal angles and insurance need to be checked.

- **Sharing your garden**
  Landshare agreements are becoming popular as there is a shortage of gardens and allotments for people who want to grow their own food. Yana and Ned take part in the Totnes Garden Share Scheme, where people who have larger gardens than they want provide space for others to work on and enjoy. There are over 100,000 people on waiting lists for spare garden space in England alone.

- **Renting your home to TV or film producers**
  Leslie made money from her house, which was used as a background for a film. Most demand is for substantial homes with good parking within the M25 for films or lifestyle photo shoots, but there is also regional demand.

Innovative schemes such as 'Homeshare' are also becoming popular. This is organised by a charity called Crossroads. It provides affordable housing in central London for young people and companionship and support for older people who live alone. One scheme participant is

Barbara Clapham, aged 97, who is supported by Beth Cooke, aged 26. Beth washes up, cooks and shops. Barbara said: 'All my contemporaries have gone, which is boring. So it's nice to have someone round the place.' Beth also benefits in non-financial ways. She enjoys living with Barbara and learns a lot about life from her. This is one creative way of providing extra accommodation and enabling older people to stay in their own homes.

Other creative solutions include living in a mobile home or caravan, or going on a cruise for a season while renting out the family home, or house swapping for holidays. Others refigure their house and let part of it as self-contained accommodation.

As you will see there are many ways, traditional and innovative, of making money on your home. Think about what might suit you best. Before rushing in it is a good idea to talk to someone who has experience of the scheme you are thinking of, so that you can get some ideas about the advantages and drawbacks.

For further information on all these schemes see the Resources section.

Raising Money on Your Home

If you don't want to downsize to raise money there are several schemes that unlock capital without you having to move. The three main types of equity release plans include reversion schemes, lifetime mortgages and home income plans. According to 'The Good Non-Retirement Guide', it is essential that the full financial and other implications are understood, and it's particularly important to ensure that there is an absolute guarantee that you can stay in your home for as long as you want. Each of these plans raises important issues.

- **Reversion schemes**
  You sell the ownership of your home to the reversion company. You will not be charged interest payments, but the money you receive from the sale will be substantially less than the current market of your home.

- **Lifetime mortgages**

  These mortgages are known as 'roll-up loans' and advance a sum of money or regular income on which you pay no interest. The interest payments are added to the original loan and are repaid from your estate on death. The disadvantage is that the compound interest can mount up quickly, leaving little or nothing for heirs to inherit.

- **Home income plans**

  These plans work on the basis of a mortgage arrangement whereby the loan is used to purchase an annuity to provide a guaranteed income for life. The interest is fixed and deducted from the annuity payment before you receive your share. These have fallen from favour as few people would derive much value and should be considered only by those well into their 80s.

In the north-west of England £51m worth of equity was released in the first six months of 2011, according to Key Retirement Solutions, an equity release specialist. The most popular schemes are the lifetime mortgages. This suggests that retirees are giving this option serious consideration for funding their income. As with all financial matters the best advice is to seek professional and independent advice before embarking on any scheme, a view echoed by all.

Closing Thoughts

Apart from the decision to downsize or stay put, there are many other options you need to think about – for example, upsizing, living abroad, finding specialist accommodation or sharing your home with others. It is important to remember that you may move more than once as your needs change over time. You might want to consider different options, such as offering accommodation in exchange for a lodger undertaking some of your household tasks. Social as well as practical outcomes accrue.

Whatever choice you make, think about your belongings and possessions and what these mean to you, and whether your home would benefit from some de-cluttering.

You might want to use some time in retirement to change, adapt and improve your living spaces, so that you can strengthen your new lifestyle and creative, social and recreational activities. Your home and garden have multiple roles and functions. They are used as places in which you can work, contemplate, entertain, socialise and carry out creative endeavours. They can also be used to raise money in various ways – all designed to support you in living your life to the full.

Chapter 11

This *Is* Your Rainy Day: Relationships with Money

It is a universal truth that retirement means less money and more time to spend it. To make matters worse, in the future many workers will receive smaller pensions than they anticipated, at a later date, and they will have to pay larger contributions towards them. It is hardly surprising that these changes have been greeted with a great deal of opposition. Pension anxiety is easy to induce with stories that draw upon the rhetoric of a demographic time bomb.

At the policy level, anxieties about the increase in costs of the growing numbers of pensioners are taken for granted. Fears are raised about the dependence of older people, as if they have made no contribution towards pensions during their working life. The demographic time bomb is made scarier by the impression that pensioners make no contribution once they leave work. For ideological or political reasons public commentators ignore their economic activity, the work they undertake, the income and other taxes paid, and their considerable contributions through both formal and informal voluntary activities. The image of the dependent and costly pensioner is not only out of date but also fuels pension anxiety.

Individuals approaching the end of their earning life are often fearful about their financial futures. For the lucky ones this is their rainy day, when their savings become a resource to realise their ambitions and plans. The demand for guidance about finances is met by books, websites, radio programmes and qualified financial advisers. Their overwhelming purpose is to maximise income for retirees. Here are just three nuggets of advice from us. Other retirees offer advice at the end of the chapter.

Seek independent and professional financial advice about your pension(s), savings, investments and other financial plans; get further advice when your circumstances change.
Seek the above advice as early as you can – well before you retire. It's never too early.
Seek advice very soon if you have not yet done so. It's never too late.

This chapter examines how our relationship with money alters in retirement. This important topic receives little attention in the published guidance or advice from professional advisers. To gather material for this chapter we asked a selection of retirees to answer some questions (see box below), so that they could inform other retirees what it was like for them. It was a very informal survey; we approached acquaintances and friends of friends who were retired and willing to tell us about their finances. We aimed for as broad a mix as we could – the well-off people as well as those in reduced circumstances; men and women; people who had worked for organisations as well as those who had been self-employed. They told us about the shifts in their relationship with money, their revised priorities and resourcefulness in finding ways to live on smaller incomes.

You might want to consider your own responses to these questions before reading what others have said. If you have not yet retired, you can use the questions to reflect on your hopes and fears for the future.

Our questions about money
How did you feel about money before you retired?
In what ways has your financial situation changed?
What adjustments have you made over time with your finances?
What, if anything, might have helped your transitions (related to money)?
What do you feel about work/paid work now?
What criteria do you use now to spend money?
What advice would you give to others?

They answered the questions but also commented how useful it was to reflect on their financial situation. It allowed them to notice the changes that had taken place and reflect, in particular, on the insights they gained during the period of adjustment to a lower income. Their honesty, courage and humour are inspiring.

Anxiety about Lower Income Decreases over Time

At the most extreme, retirees moved from panic to confidence as they learned how to deal with their money over time. They used words such as 'panic', 'worry', 'scary', 'insecurity' and 'anxiety' to describe their anticipation of a lower income. Others were reassured that they were not as badly off as they had anticipated because their outgoings were also reduced (e.g., if their mortgage has been paid off). Others thought ahead about the implications, and actively prepared for the income reduction by making adjustments in advance (e.g., purchasing items for later use while still earning).

Charlotte, describing herself as in an acute state of panic before leaving work, reported that she now felt confident and even relaxed about how she was managing:

I knew I could always adjust my lifestyle to match my incomings as I had always done in the past but something got in the way of that rational thinking – panic, I think it was. So I just had to experience it … Now I really enjoy the task of managing my budget. I get a little thrill of pride. I enjoy money now as I find it is liberating. I perceive money differently. Before I retired I saw it as paying the bills and now I see it as a way to live my life. I have respect for money. I don't waste it. I see it as a resource.

Many of our retirees adjusted to the reduction in their incomes with relative ease. Even those, like Joseph, who had a very low income, did not appear to be unhappy as a result, because money now is more reliable. Joseph explained:

When I was working I was earning a modest but adequate salary but it was always insecure. Now I am retired and on state benefits, money is much tighter, but it is secure, which allows me to plan ahead, and to pace myself. But this has thrown me back on my own resources, and I have learned to appreciate so many little things that are around all of us.

Mike reflected on how his grandparents and others in their generation managed in their retirement. While his situation is very different, being much more affluent, he is still financially cautious:

Their only income was the state pension, and their lifestyle expectations were very limited. I've also recalled an article I read about 50 years ago when I was serving my apprenticeship. A journeyman who had retired wrote that he was now tending his garden, and wearing out his old clothes. All being working-class Victorians this is hardly surprising. Strange then for me to be thinking that despite much progress and optimism in our age, including, for example, longer life expectancy, greater access to a wide range of culture and easy transport, nevertheless worries about limited income and being financially cautious seem to be just as prevalent. On the other hand it makes sense that to be able to take advantage of the benefits of the social advantages existing now it's essential to have a reasonable income. If not, the potential frustrations of living without being able to afford a reasonable social life could be worse than those earlier retired generations who didn't expect one in the first place.

The ability of retirees to adjust to lower incomes is in part because big purchases (e.g., houses, cars, family holidays) have usually been completed by the time of their retirement. As a result their priorities have changed. It is striking that, according to research published in the *Guardian* in 2012, people are generally happier in their 60s and 70s than they were in their 40s and 50s. It was suggested that older people have learned how to cope with hardship and negative circumstances, and that they may have lowered their expectations.

Taking a gradual approach to retirement helped retirees learn to cope with a decreased amount of money. Mavis explained that she would not have coped very well with a sudden drop in her income, but she adjusted well to its gradual reduction:

It took me years to work things out, to make some longer-term purchases while still working, and most importantly to really accept that I would be among the poorer section of society as an older woman. Having come from a financially poor background really helped, as I knew how to manage on less money and still enjoy life to the full.

Even if people became less panicked, worries about limited income were nonetheless prevalent across the whole survey, even for those who seem financially very secure. Mike said:

I have a recurring concern that we may face major house repair costs, which could lead to a decision to move before any such problems arise (we have also thought about moving due to reasons of disability) … The issue everyone faces is possible disability, and the need for sheltered housing or nursing care.

Shami was another person who mentioned apprehension about house repairs and health issues. She added that dental work is a major expense as one gets older, as is the cost of a decent pair of glasses. She was also worried about the cost of visiting her family in Canada and Sri Lanka, pointing out that as well as fares the travel insurance is exorbitant.

But Mavis demonstrated a way in which older people can raise income from their assets after their retirement, drawing attention to the benefits in having owned property: 'Downsizing is brilliant and releases treat money and boosts meagre savings. As does equity release.'

These examples demonstrate the different ways in which anxiety reduces over time. If you are feeling panicky, stressed or anxious about general money matters or managing on a lower income, remember that these feelings may be temporary. There are things you can do. Notice what you are feeling and why, and then discuss your situation with a friend, colleague or financial adviser. Talking with others can be calming and is likely to help you see a way forward.

Changing Spending Priorities

All the retirees faced reductions in their incomes – some to a half of what they used to receive before. A few were receiving state benefits and no occupational pensions. They were all required to prioritise their expenditure and change their spending behaviour. 'I'm still learning – it's a very hard thing to do,' Shami reported.

Overall, those who responded to our questions indicated a hierarchy of spending priorities:

1. essentials;
2. social and family contacts;

3. health and fitness; and
4. treats.

Essential expenditures included meeting physical needs, heating, food and other unavoidable expenses. Shami, surviving on a small income, reported being careful with unavoidable outgoings, checking the value of everything and paying attention to every possible saving – for example, through using direct debit payments for utility bills and buying items when they were on special offer. Some, like Annie, reported that the cost of essentials can be reduced in other ways:

> I sold my car, signed up for my Freedom Pass and Senior Rail Card, and I ask for senior reductions in galleries, etc. I try to limit spontaneous purchases of books, clothes and CDs. I eat out much less, eat less, and generally try to be more careful.

Joseph laconically reported surviving by 'skipping on luxuries'.

Social connections, including families, came next in importance: enjoying time with family and friends, sharing food, outings, providing for family members, etc. Financial changes altered relationships with friends and family, and possibly reduced the degree of financial generosity. However, retirees reported that they made appropriate adaptations, such as having their social life based more in their own homes, sharing food and engaging in more informal activities. Having more time can be an advantage here.

Retirees who were parents talked about changes in how they provided for their children and grandchildren. They regretted being unable to provide so generously for them, but still made them a priority. Jasper said:

> The arrival of grandchildren has had a significant effect on our resources as we have decided to hand over substantial amounts from our savings to our two sons.

Mavis had carefully planned how to alter her outgoings, but reported:

> A downside of the adjustment was being unable to help out grandchildren as much as before, with pocket money and treats; that took a lot of thought and planning how to 'give' as much as before, but not financially.

Some were continuing to invest money for their grandchildren, while others regretted being unable to save as much as they wanted for them.

Those who do not have children had a different attitude to the disposal of their property and money. Charlotte commented:

> Making a will is important and someone once told me to write mine, to reflect who I am and what I value. This is even more important for people who have children. I don't have children or any really close relatives, apart from my partner, and I think that makes a huge difference to how you see your assets as you grow older. I don't want any money left unless it is to give to my partner so that she is comfortable when she gets older. She is younger so I expect she will live longer than me.

Family connections work both ways as Christopher's poignant story reveals:

> My transition into bankruptcy has been greatly helped by the support of my sons and daughter and other family members. I have always known that they would not allow me to be truly homeless (I did have over a year in a caravan) or hungry. Furthermore state benefits have been a godsend … I did feel guilty about relying on the state now, but as good friends have said to me that is what they pay taxes for and they are quite happy with that.

The third spending priority for retirees was health and fitness. Annie reported on her adjustments as follows.

> I have cut down on food, books, little treats, but I still go to expensive Pilates, save for holidays, give to charities, save for my grandchildren, etc … I have some priorities that I have chosen to invest in: my own health and fitness, travel to the West Country and accommodation there (to look after grandchildren and be near family), savings for holidays, modest treats, etc.

Even with reduced incomes, treats featured in the answers – the fourth spending priority. Jasper explained:

> We do not replace cars like we used to, but we don't stint on holidays … Now we have done as much as we can for our children and grandchildren, we are determined to enjoy as much travel as possible while our health is still good.

An excellent story came from Mavis, who, despite having a reduced fixed income, reported:

> I still treat myself every day. Try the one-third of a bottle size of good champagne, you can get them in packs of four very reasonably – two of these packs go in with the weekly supermarket shop so I can honestly say now I have a bottle of champagne every day.

Others spoke of how they use money to continue to lead a stimulating life, including visits to plays, films, concerts, live music and dance events.

Retirees learned that obstacles can be overcome and that expensive presents can be replaced with creative, sometimes homemade and more thoughtful alternatives, which may turn out to be more personal and therefore more cherished.

These experiences are reported to help you think about your situation and what adjustments you can make to your spending priorities. Think about your hierarchy and compare it to the one that emerged from the analysis of those surveyed: essentials, social and family contacts, health and fitness, and treats.

Clarification of Values for Expenditure

An outcome of changing priorities was that it clarified the values that the retirees interviewed held dear and wanted to live by. The most obvious was in relation to other people, in particular families, as Christopher reported:

> Surprisingly, I find that I am happier now than I have ever been in my life, even though I have nothing … Money is only a tool and not a God … Money has never been an object in life for me. It has only ever been a means to an end … I have renewed contact with most of my family and friends (difficult before because of being committed to a livestock farm), and am free to do that which I wish on a daily basis.

Our respondents manage their money in ways that support their values, in particular their desire to act responsibly towards themselves and others. They are now choosing to use their money to produce less waste, to be more environmentally aware and to make healthier choices. Annie explained her position: 'I generally try to be less profligate. It fits my ethic of behaving responsibly towards the planet's resources as well.' This approach was reinforced by Joseph:

> You can do greater good by the way you spend money, which is the whole point of the ethical consumer movement, fair trade, etc … Although money does not determine our happiness, it is absolutely imperative to have a correct attitude to it, being as it is a limiting factor.

Having described many difficulties, sacrifices and strategies with her small pension, Shami said:

> Finally, all this does not mean to say being stingy and selfish. All this is in a framework of generosity and selflessness, that is, not forgetting others and sharing one's time, energy and what one has with others.

The importance of making decisions based on values emerges strongly. When you think about these accounts, consider how in retirement our respondents were able to reflect their values in their expenditures.

Attitudes to Paid and Unpaid Employment

The question about work in retirement provoked strong responses. Joseph, for example, believed that retirees shouldn't give up making a contribution to the wider world through unpaid work, echoing Shami's comments about avoiding selfishness.

> It is dangerous to think retirement is a fabulous time when you just do whatever pleases you. It is important to feel you are still contributing to the common good, by voluntary work or whatever.

Mavis rejected work outright.

> I refuse to go back to work to buy THINGS. I wouldn't go near it! I remember the delight I felt in finishing my very last assignment, and receiving my last pay cheque. Others may find they miss work and the money, but I don't. I don't feel I have lost any self-esteem or value or social networks you get at work either, but I put this down to the gradual run down which I had; it enabled me to have the time for thought, planning and discussion.

The retirees who are still involved in paid work reported undertaking it for its intrinsic pleasure or for the social aspects. They chose work that was stimulating, interesting, challenging and worthwhile, where they had respect and admiration for the people or organisations that employed them. This was also apparent in their choice of work when it concerned issues reflecting their values or when they continued to use their skills. They were often very selective about how they did this. Jasper works now and then but limits himself to giving advice based on his experience, rather than taking on big projects. Money earned was seen by our retirees as a bonus and used to purchase luxuries, the occasional and exotic treats. Annie said:

> I like to have some income for paid work coming in. It doesn't have to be a great deal. I can justify indulgences, or buying certain items of clothes this way. The things I really like doing (writing, coaching) I'll do for peanuts.

Some retirees went even further in their attitude to paid employment. For example, Charlotte said that she likes *not* getting paid for what she does as a volunteer, suggesting that this makes a big difference. 'In counselling and befriending it is so valuable for clients to know that people are helping them and not getting anything for that work.'

Many of our retirees prioritised unpaid childcare. In Shami's case, not only has she prioritised her grandsons, but she believes that she should also make way for younger people who need to make a living:

> I do not always feel able to work at present as my commitments are to my family – with two young grandsons I feel I should be readily available to support them with my time. In due course I may take up voluntary work. Although it would be great to get some additional income, as someone able to 'manage' I feel paid work should be left to a younger person who is trying to find a living.

Charlotte was disappointed to find that other people's attitudes to her changed when she took up paid work again. They held her in higher esteem because she works in a prestigious organisation rather than being retired and not working:

> That says a lot, I think, about the value people attach to you if they know a) that you are 'working for money' and b) work in a prestigious organisation. I am surprised by people's reactions when I tell them about this consultancy. They sit up and take notice as if my life is more important. I think it's a shame that this makes such a difference to how others see me and about how I see myself. It is sad that people value you more when you are in work more than being retired.

You may have strong views about the place of paid or unpaid work in your life and the reasons for doing it. You may have no choice as your income may be insufficient to cover your outgoings and you have to continue to earn money. Or you may want to work to provide interest, purpose, companionship and prestige, or to satisfy your work ethic rather than as a financial imperative. On the other hand you may be in a position to forget all about paid work and relax and enjoy your freedom, and find lots of new ways to gain satisfaction and purpose, including non-paid work. Whatever you choose, remember you can try things out for a while and then change your mind. No decision is irrevocable.

Don't Panic: Guidance and Advice from Retirees

People who have learned about finances from the experience of retirement over several years offer two pieces of advice:

1. **Don't panic** was their overriding message. As Joseph explained, you don't need a lot of money to be happy, but you do need to be satisfied with what you have.

2. **Think ahead** was a message that came across strongly in the different accounts. Planning what you want to get from your money is crucial, as Mavis suggested (e.g., buying expensive things while you are still earning).

Jasper spoke about the importance of choosing the right financial adviser. 'The selection of an independent financial adviser should be done with the utmost care. Getting this right could mean a reasonable result, getting it wrong could lead to disaster.'

Charlotte came up with a list of advice saying, 'I was pleased when I read an article in *Choice* magazine on simplifying your finances as I had done most of the things they recommended.' Here are her suggestions:

1. Use cash so you are aware of what you are spending. Have one credit card for emergencies and pay it before interest is added. Use direct debits for bills.
2. Continue monitoring your spending. Review your regular incomings and outgoings annually to work out what's left over. Use what's left for important things rather than frittering it away.
3. Keep careful records and file papers consistently so your tax return is easier to complete.
4. Enjoy your money and make it work for you to have the best time you can.
5. Stop saving: this *is* your rainy day. Ensure you spend or give away all your money before you die.

Consider what would be in your list, perhaps by thinking about what sort of advice you would give to a friend.

Closing Thoughts

The overwhelming picture emerging from these responses is that retirees, having more confidence, wisdom and experience, are managing their money in ways that support their values and their desire to act responsibly towards themselves and others.

Generosity is not limited to money, as Shami suggested, and you can be generous in the use of your other resources, such as your time, company, kindness and wisdom. While you may have to be less generous financially with gifts or financial contributions to the lives of friends and family, they may appreciate you in different ways if you share your other resources with them. Mavis also observed that planning financial aspects of retirement 'goes hands together with all elements of your old-ageing'.

Financial resources impact upon many areas of your life. They can cause stress or allow you opportunities for great pleasures, but can only be the means to an end.

Chapter 12

Wonder and Awe:
The Time of Your Life

Dunbar is one of the most intriguing and compelling characters in Joseph Heller's novel *Catch-22*. Dunbar serves in the US Air Force with the main character of the novel, Yossarian, and together they are trapped on the fictional Mediterranean island of Pianosa during the latter days of the second world war. Transfixed by the idea that death is inches away when they fly their missions, Dunbar attempts to make time go slowly by filling it with boredom. He likes being with people who annoy him, and the game of skeet, because he hates them so much that they make time pass more slowly. When challenged to explain why anyone would want a life filled with boredom he replies, 'What else is there?' Dunbar, facing the limits of his life, sees the passing of time as a threat requiring boredom to slow it down.

Dunbar is a poor model for having the time of your life. He should have listened to Abraham Lincoln who is reported to have said: 'And in the end, it's not the years in your life that count. It's the life in your years.' Or perhaps to Montaigne, from the 16th century, who wrote something similar: 'The value of life lies not in the length of days, but in the use we make of them.'

Before they retire people are frequently asked about how they will spend their time. There is an implication that it will be a problem, intensified by the idea that if you don't do something now you never will. This chapter is not about packing your retirement years with holidays, crosswords and running marathons. Rather, it is about taking the opportunity to benefit from the experience and wisdom of maturity to find and enjoy an added dimension: wonder and awe. You should resist the example of Dunbar and experience the time of your life.

After nearly half a century spent in the service of others, now is the chance to focus on what's important and valuable to you. The most wonderful experiences need not cost a great deal, nor do you need to travel for them.

Wonder and Awe Unwrapped

'These sweet moments are what life's all about,' said one retiree when asked about experiences of wonder and awe. Here are some moments reported to us:

- **John:** 'Watching my grandson score his first goal in the school football team. I was fit to burst.'
- **Isobel:** 'Seeing a polar bear playing in the snow. I'll never forget the moment.'
- **Clive:** 'Spotting a crane, whenever I do I still get a bit potty over such a graceful bird.'
- **Stella:** 'Singing at the Albert Hall with a scratch choir. The sound was fantastic.'
- **Betty:** 'Watching Carlos Acosta and Sarah Lamb dance at the Royal Opera House in a thrilling production of Poulenc's *Gloria*. Magical.'
- **Frank:** 'Sailing my new dinghy with my partner. What a thrill!'
- **Jack:** 'The Grand Canyon – it took my breath away.'
- **Jo:** 'Running my first half-marathon. The time wasn't that good but that didn't matter.'
- **Winston:** 'Watching the sunset on a ferry on the way to the Shetland Isles. The best I have ever seen.'

- **Ruby:** 'Downsizing my car to a tiny bright red second-hand convertible on my 65th birthday. The wind in my hair as I drove home made me feel 30 again.'
- **Dan:** 'Seeing 15 ducklings on the canal in October. I couldn't believe my eyes.'
- **Chris:** 'Renewing our vows on our golden wedding anniversary with all the family gathered together in the church we married in.'
- **Tom:** 'Listening and dancing to the music of the Ultimate Eagles. I was right in the moment, felt uplifted and happy.'
- **Maggie:** 'Sitting in the sunshine in my garden after coming out of hospital following a major operation. The warmth on my skin was amazing.'

In these diverse experiences we notice the heightened and strong emotional responses. The occasions of wonder and awe are out of the ordinary, infrequent, may be planned or spontaneous, and may tell you something about your existence in the world. These experiences are sometimes about the relationship of a person to something on a larger scale. This relationship may be to natural phenomena (e.g., the Grand Canyon), aesthetic skill (e.g., the ballet), or the strength of love (e.g., with family and other loved ones). All the responses are to do with the relationship of the individual to other people or things. We can see that there is an awareness of one or more of the following:

- insignificance or smallness in relation to the world – the Grand Canyon experience;
- connections to other living things – in the presence of wildlife or in wilderness areas;
- connections to family and other people – pride in grandchildren, celebrating a long and happy marriage with family, sailing with a partner, singing in a choir;
- responses to being alive – especially after serious illness or in circumstances of heightened awareness; and
- senses – singing, dancing, the wind in one's hair, the sun on one's skin.

The people who told us about their experiences did not find it hard to describe their moments of wonder and awe. You may wish to consider what comes to your mind. But what is meant by these words? Perhaps wonder and awe exist on a continuum with awe as an extreme expression of wonder? The characteristics of wonder include surprise, unexpectedness, novelty and beauty. If awe is a heightened form of wonder then it may be characterised by astonishment, reverence and veneration.

But why wonder and awe are important in life is not clearly understood. One view is that as well as the human desire and motivation to be always learning, there is a similar human yearning to explore, travel, discover new and wonderful things, and be amazed.

Wonder and Awe and Connections with Spiritual Experiences

Wonder and awe are closely associated with spiritual experiences. They nurture the spiritual aspects of life, as opposed to material or physical things. While spirituality can be associated with religion and many people find spirituality in religious experiences, this chapter is concerned with spirituality outside any formalised religious practices or beliefs, a kind of secular spirituality.

There are several definitions of spirituality. These include:

- a belief in a power operating in the universe that is greater than oneself;
- a sense of interconnectedness with all living creatures;
- an awareness of purpose and meaning in life; and
- the development of personal values.

The idea of interconnectedness is central, says our colleague Ron Best, a professor who explored spiritual education in his professional life. Spiritual experience is to be fully human, fully alive and wholly at one with another, to love and be loved. He says:

… it is rich in affect or feeling, but is not reducible to emotion. It is holistic, involving our bodies and our senses as much as our emotions, and it occurs within personal relationships characterised by trust … and in which the experience of two persons is not a means to an end but infinitely valued in itself.

Secular spirituality is associated with the struggle to understand existential issues – how our lives fit into the greater scheme of things, wondering where the universe comes from, why we are here, or what happens when we die. The practice of spiritual development includes meditation, contemplation and reading poetry.

It's also true that spiritual experiences occur within everyday activities. For example, when researcher Kathryn Copsey ran an after-school club for five- to 11-year-olds she observed: a sense of adventure, spontaneity, imagination, gentleness, joy and wonder in small things, candour, trust, innocence, generosity. Young people were experiencing these despite the context of formal education and socialisation processes that may sometimes impede spiritual development. In retirement your life can be full of everyday spiritual experiences similar to those Kathryn observed in young people, such as openness to feelings and other people, a sense of immediacy, and freedom of spirit. You can:

- find wonder in everything, seek out what is new, unknown or not understood;
- express feelings, rather than repress them;
- stay focused and live in the now;
- take the ordinary and make it extraordinary;
- appreciate what is simple and uncomplicated;
- make something out of nothing, spend time playfully;
- use objects to inspire thoughts of other times and other places;
- see life as integrated, rather than make distinctions between the ordinary and the extraordinary; and
- love, show love and be loved; remember you have an endless capacity for it.

Retirees are often struck by how they return to the sort of activities they enjoyed when they were much younger – creative activities such as painting or making music, as well as physical activities such as sports, dancing or walking. During your working life you may not have had the time or space in your head to engage with such activities. In retirement you may find the time and inclination to reconsider how you live your life in relation to spiritual experiences and the values you hold.

Seeking Wonder, Awe and Spiritual Experience through Travel

While your life can be full of everyday spiritual experiences, you may seek longer, more drawn-out experiences – often through special journeys. Travel is a useful topic to explore how our desire for wonder, awe and spiritual experiences can be satisfied.

The idea of pilgrimage as a source of spiritual experience has a long history. Followers of many religions have included pilgrimage as part of their spiritual disciplines. For centuries, Muslims have journeyed to Mecca, Jews to Jerusalem and Christians to holy places. One pilgrimage destination, Canterbury Cathedral, was immortalised by Chaucer in *The Canterbury Tales*. Specific routines in pilgrimages included preparation, journeying, time spent in prayer and meditation, then slowly returning outward, bringing back a renewed and revived spirit.

The idea of pilgrimage, making a transformative journey to a sacred centre, remains a powerful metaphor for restoring spiritual life. Satish Kumar, the conservationist who made an 8,000-mile peace walk in his youth, still extols the importance of walking to restore reverence in nature. The title of his autobiography, *No Destination*, is a reminder that it's the journey that is significant. Quoting the philosopher Nietzsche, 'never trust a thought that didn't come by walking', he refers to the power of walking to connect to the natural world:

When you walk, you are in touch with the earth, with nature, the wasps, the insects, everything. In a car or a train or a plane, you are disconnected. You walk to connect yourself.

While they may not refer to their travels as a pilgrimage, retirees often seek a non-religious alternative to rediscover the transforming potential of travel, of leaving the familiar behind and seeking out places that have special spiritual significance, experiencing places in quietude and contemplation, becoming refreshed, and returning renewed and transformed. Such journeys, even when they are not undertaken on foot, remove you from everyday responsibilities and distractions, leaving behind the ordinary to travel to the exotic, in order to reassess what is and what isn't significant.

Life in the mature years is being redefined by a major social revolution, as many retirees undertake activities denied to them when younger. It's not surprising that after 30–40 years tied by careers, jobs and families, being controlled by the clock and timetables, retirees decide to escape the predictability of routine and set off to explore the world. Ros Altman, director general of *Saga* magazine, reported that typically this includes going to far-flung destinations, visiting the Himalayas or trekking through Borneo. Such adventures can include danger.

One British couple, Bruce Scott (62) and Lesley Norris (64), attracted press attention when they were rescued by helicopter from the Brazilian Amazon after their camper van fell into a ravine. They had spent four years travelling across Latin America, having swapped their lives in London for adventures in 2006. Lesley had worked for British Airways for 20 years. Bruce, a photographer, said they wanted to indulge their mutual passion for travelling. He sold his studio flat to buy an off-road vehicle, which became their home. Lesley had spent a year learning Spanish in preparation.

Rather than travel independently with the associated risks (such as Bruce and Lesley experienced), retirees often take guided tours – they go on safaris, set sail to see the Northern Lights, visit the pyramids in Egypt, fly over the Grand Canyon, explore the

Galapagos or spend months on cruise ships. A huge industry exists to support these adventures.

Age is a consideration as Jennie told us. As a former historian she is planning to go to faraway places of great historical importance while she is still able to cope with long-haul flights. The carbon cost of such trips may present a dilemma. Martin Dunford, publishing director of Rough Guides, maintains that most of the time the benefits far outweigh the drawbacks. He argues that a world made up of nations that keep themselves to themselves would be a less interesting and, perhaps, a more dangerous place; that our planet is rich and diverse; that it is one of the pleasures of life to see and understand as much as we can. We can make the most of our time on earth through travel, he claims.

The joy of travel, and with it some moments of pure wonder and awe, has become available to most people in the last 50 years. The former Archbishop of Canterbury Robert Runcie said: 'I sometimes think that Thomas Cook should be numbered among the secular saints. He took travel from the privileged and gave it to the people.'

There are many ways of visiting or living in remote places other than as tourists. Silver Gappers take a year out to travel when they retire. Volunteering provides great possibilities (e.g., Voluntary Service Overseas), and there are shorter-term contracts for older people who have specific expertise (e.g., school management).

Your resources may be a deciding factor when it comes to travel. But you may have prioritised your rainy-day money to spend on holidays, perhaps blowing your lump sum on a world cruise, or planning exciting trips on a very limited budget. The success of the over-60s' free bus pass has meant that thousands of retirees pursue excitement and wonder at little cost.

Two retired friends travelled from the Scottish border to Land's End, Cornwall, in 2008 – by bus. The journey took eight days and covered 552 miles on 33 different buses – and it didn't cost a penny. Sally Clarke (68) and Fran Taylor (71) raised £3,000 in sponsorship towards the cost of replacing the heating system at their local church in Norwich. Sally said: 'The trip has been a fantastic experience. We have had a chance to see some beautiful places and scenery and to catch up with friends and family.' Former education training officer Fran, a widowed grandmother of 10, added: 'We thought we ought to show people we were prepared to do something to raise money rather than just going round with a collection box.' On the way they celebrated Fran's birthday outside Exeter Cathedral, and stayed in B&Bs and with family or friends.

Sally and Fran experienced awe and wonder from the different landscapes, architecture and social contact, and realised a great sense of achievement and pleasure. They moved from the familiar, were challenged and had fun.

Finding wilderness areas to lift your spirits can be achieved near to home by walking in woods, by a river or reservoir, and even in the heart of cities. Satish, who we talked about earlier, lives in north Devon, and despite his history of long walks also finds inspiration close to home:

> On your doorstep are the most extraordinary places. The ordinary is extraordinary here. When my wife asked what I would like to do for my birthday, I said I only wanted to go to Dartmoor. When I want inspiration or new thinking, I go there.

This view is echoed by Martin Dunford from Rough Guides:

> It's possible to have some of the best travel experiences without going very far at all. Travel isn't only about distance and long-haul flights. However, the most meaningful often take place when we move away from the familiar, out of our comfort zone, where even the most run-of-the-mill situations and events take on an exotic quality.

Even those who live in cities can find wonder and awe in the natural world close to home. Dan saw the October ducklings on the canal near his house. Caroline walked the London Outer Orbital Path inside the M25 and frequently walks in or close to London, enjoying the natural world, from blackberries to panoramic views.

The Achievement of Ambitions, Goals and Dreams

Many challenge the idea of making and achieving goals for the sake of it, and instead give priority to the learning that accrues from reflection. Goals have their place, indeed they are useful as a starting point, but they are limited because the complexities of thought processes and behaviour are sometimes overlooked. It is far more important to be learning-centred than goal-driven.

Nevertheless, an important activity in retiring groups and on courses is the setting of short-term and long-term goals, and voicing ambitions and dreams. It is good to review them and celebrate achievements or, in some cases, help yourself and others to understand why some goals haven't been met. From this you may discover that you have been ambivalent about some forms of action, the goals may have been inappropriate or that other events have overtaken you. Reviewing and redefining goals can lead to important learning. Goals highlight the importance of looking ahead and making good use of your time.

Inspirational narratives have informed this book and the list below highlights some of the many goals, ambitions and dreams achieved.

- **Allie:** Five years living in France – achieving a lifelong ambition.
- **Dave:** Ballroom dancing three nights a week with a new partner.
- **Christina:** Lost 20 stone in the four-year period since she retired and has reached her target weight.
- **Sophie:** Completed her first novel.
- **Beatrice:** Glad she has moved to a smaller house.
- **Ann:** Happy in a new full-time career as a teacher of English as a foreign language.
- **Alan and Carol:** Given a home to a rescued dog.
- **Ken:** Re-read the complete works of Dickens on his Kindle.
- **Monica:** Got a group together to protest about their local library closing down.

- **Steph:** Joined a choir and performs regularly at the local care centre.
- **Felicity:** Learned to knit and crochet and made wonderful presents.
- **Sonia:** Heard her short story read on the radio.

Identifying goals or dreams publicly can be an important step towards achieving them. Drawing on others for support is helpful too. The film *The Bucket List* is a good example. Here two men with nothing in common, except their terminal illness, decide to do all the things they ever wanted to do before they 'kick the bucket'. In the process they become unlikely friends and find joy in life. They try skydiving, climbing the pyramids, driving a Shelby Mustang, flying over the North Pole, eating dinner at Le Chèvre d'Or in France and visiting the Taj Mahal. Their less obvious ambitions may be more appealing: to laugh till they cried, to help a complete stranger for the good and to witness something truly majestic.

In 2011, in a special edition of the BBC Radio 4 *Woman's Hour* on becoming older, one guest reported the marking of her 60th birthday. She compiled 60 new things to do in the coming year – things she had never tried in her life before. These were fun, tangible goals. Other less concrete, yet significant achievements include everyday things like making time to talk with neighbours. A serious, yet funny ambition suggested by one retiree who felt her life was too structured, was to plan to be more spontaneous. Occasionally, you need to seize the moment, be open to new experiences and be free from routines, goals or plans if they become restrictive.

The potential to experience wonder and awe, and the connections with spirituality, are evident in the goals reported above. Enrich your life in ways that are appealing to you.

Closing Thoughts

In living through the transitions of retiring and retirement, it would be good to claim that:

1. I have the courage to live a life true to myself, not the life others expect of me.
2. I am enjoying the activities in which I now want to engage.
3. I have the courage to express my feelings.
4. I have stayed in touch with my closest friends and family, and have reconnected with those I now have time to see.
5. I let myself be as happy as I can be.

These statements are positive adaptations of the regrets reported in an article about palliative nurse Bronnie Ware's book, *The Top Five Regrets of the Dying*. You probably want your retirement to hold few regrets. In keeping with the themes of this book, consider how it would be possible to pre-empt such regrets and live more as you would like. Start celebrating your life rather than mulling over regrets, and identify what you still want to achieve.

Nor do you want to be thinking 'I am not the sort of person who does that sort of thing' when confronted with a new experience. Retirees who hold this view are severely restricted by their narrow views of themselves. As an older person you can develop a new identity and redefine your life. Take inspiration from the influential American psychologist Carl Rogers, who was still a practitioner at 78. He reflected on how much he had enjoyed the previous 10 years and said he had been able to:

> ... open myself to new ideas, new feelings and new risks ... Increasingly I discover that being alive involves taking a chance, acting on less than certainty, engaging with life. All this brings change and for me the process of change is life. I realise that if I were stable and static it would be a living death.

The message is to be open to new ideas, new feelings and new risks.

We are off now to have the time of our lives and recommend that you do too.

Resources

On Support

Cussen, M, 'Journey through the 6 Stages of Retirement' (2009)
www.investopedia.com/articles/retirement/07/sixstages.asp

Life Academy – for personal coaching and training techniques
www.life-academy.co.uk

Retirement Online – online retirement groups
www.retirement-online.com/online-retirement-groups.html

Retiring on a Literal Shoestring: Support Group
www.city-data.com/forum/retirement/653489-retiring-literal-shoe-string-support-group.html

On Relationships, Conflict and Communication

Improving Your World – overcoming tension in relationships (16
December 2008)
www.improvingyourworld.com/relationships/overcoming_tension_
in_relationships_002999.html

Kay, F, *The Good Non-Retirement Guide* (Kogan Page, 2011)

Relate – common problems of older people
www.relate.org.uk/relationship-help/help-older-people

Scott, E, 'Communicate: Improve Your Relationships with Effective Communication Skills' (2010)
http://stress.about.com/od/relationships/ht/healthycomm.htm

Scott, E, 'Relationship Stress: Marriage, Relationship Skills & Social Support' (2010)
http://stress.about.com/od/relationships

On Communities and Social Networks

Campaign to End Loneliness – ending loneliness and creating connections in older age
www.campaigntoendloneliness.org.uk

In My Prime – Computing made easy for the over-50s
http://inmyprime.wordpress.com/category/silver-surfers

Richmond Villages
www.richmond-villages.com

totally4women – community and network for women
www.totally4women.com

UK National Statistics
www.statistics.gov.uk

On Health and Well-Being

Action for Happiness
www.actionforhappiness.org

'Diabetes, Heart Disease, and Stroke'
http://diabetes.niddk.nih.gov/dm/pubs/stroke/#prevent

Draw Your Emotions. Developed by the Hillview Learning Disability Clinic Community Treatment Team in Sunderland from an idea by Margot Sunderland.
Contact: Denise Johnson at hoodfrog@blueyonder.co.uk or Jill Chaplin at Hillview Clinic, Sunderland SR2 9JT.

Kaiser Health News – better health during older age
www.kaisernetwork.org

New Economics Foundation – elements of well-being
www.neweconomics.org

NHS website – health advice
www.nhs.uk

On Your Home and Living Accommodation

Freecycle – changing the world one gift at a time
www.uk.freecycle.org

Green, J, Betts, J, and Wilson, C, *An Experiment in Living: Sharing a House in Later Life* (Third Age Press, 1999)
This book is out of print. However, the full text is available from Third Age Press as an A4 transcript. Cost £5. Address: 6 Parkside Gardens, London SW19 5EY.

Johnson, P, *The Armchair Naturalist: How to Be Good at Nature without Really Trying* (Icon Books, 2007)

Kay, F, *The Good Non-Retirement Guide* (Kogan Page, 2011)

Landshare – connecting growers to people with land to share
www.landshare.net

Lavish Locations – film and TV location agency
www.lavishlocations.com

Leisure Buildings
www.leisurebuildings.com

On Volunteering

Do-it – advertises a range of volunteering opportunities, including trustee roles; a good place to register your interest and find a match with local opportunities
www.do-it.org.uk

Gap Advice
www.gapadvice.org

The Guardian *Guide to Volunteering* (*Guardian* Newspapers, 2007)

Reach – for skilled volunteers, matching their skills to the needs of voluntary organisations
www.reach.org.uk

The Trustee Bank on the National Council for Voluntary Organisations – check out the 'Good Trustee Guide'
www.ncvo-vol.org.uk/trusteebank

Volunteering in Berlin
www.geb-london.org

Worldwide Volunteering
www.wwv.org.uk

Other sources:

Local authorities often have resources of information about opportunities for volunteering in the local community, from befriending older people to environmental projects that need labour. Information can be found on their individual websites.

The local **Council for Voluntary Service** can help match individuals to vacant trustee roles.

Companies may encourage potential trustees by promoting trustee work opportunities, as well as other voluntary activities, as part of a deliberate policy to assist with older workers' transitions out of work.

There are frequent **special campaigns** to recruit trustees, such as Devon's Trustee Awareness Week.

Bibliography

Throughout the book we have drawn on:

Carnell, E, and Lodge, C, *Retiring Lives* (London: Institute of Education, University of London, 2009)

Personal stories found in *Saga* magazine, *Choice*, the *Guardian*, other national publications and the BBC news website (www.bbc.co.uk/news)

Other stories have come from unpublished sources and we have changed names to guarantee confidentiality

Introduction

Bingham, J, 'Take Less, Bishop Tells Baby Boomers' (*Daily Telegraph*, 11 June 2013); www.telegraph.co.uk/news/religion/10113694/Take-less-bishop-tells-baby-boomers.html

Bottero, W, 'Gender and the Labour Market at the Turn of the Century: Complexity, Ambiguity and Change' in *Work, Employment and Society* (2000; 14: (4); pp 781–791)

Cox, A, *Age of Opportunity: Older People, Volunteering and the Big Society* (ResPublica, 2011)

Ford, R, 'This Writing Life' (*Guardian*, 29 April 2011); www.theguardian.com/books/2011/apr/29writing-life-richard-ford-author

Office of National Statistics, 'Young Adults Living with Parents in the UK' (2014); www.ons.gov.uk

van der Heide, I, van Rijn, RM, Robroek, S, Burdorf, A, and Proper, KI, 'Is Retirement Good for Your Health? A Systematic

Review of Longitudinal Studies' (*BMC Public Health*, 2013);
www.biomedcentral.com/1471-2458/13/1180

Walker, A, 'The New Ageism' in *The Political Quarterly* (2012; 83:
(4); pp 812–819)

Willetts, D, *The Pinch: How the Baby Boomers Took Their Children's
Future – And Why They Should Give it Back* (Atlantic Books,
2010)

Chapter 1: Retirement Ain't What It Used to Be
Demographic changes and the impact on retirement

Chesworth, N, 'Baby Boomers Widen Skills Gap' (*Evening Standard*,
17 May 2011)

Department for Work & Pensions, 'Over Ten Million People to Live
to 100' (30 December 2010)

Office for National Statistics, '2011 Census: Population Estimates for
the United Kingdom' (2012)

Parry, J, and Taylor, RF, 'Orientation, Opportunity and Autonomy:
Why People Work after State Pension Age in Three Areas of
England' in *Ageing and Society* (2007; 27; pp 579–598)

Pensions Policy Institute, 'Report on the Implications of the Coalition Government's Public Service Pension Reforms' (May 2013)

Scott, J, Dex, S, Joshi, H, Purcell, K, and Elias, P, 'Introduction'
in Scott, J, Dex, S, and Joshi, H (eds) *Women and Employment:
Changing Lives and New Challenges* (Edward Elgar, 2008)

Retirees' contributions

ResPublica, 'Older People "Undervalued" in the Big Society'
(ResPublica, 10 October 2011); www.respublica.org.uk/item/
Older-people-undervalued-in-the-Big-Society-says-new-report-
from-Phillip-Blond-s-think-tank

Wheeler, B, 'Lord Bichard: Retired People Could Do Work for
Pensions' (24 October 2012); www.bbc.co.uk/news/uk-politics-
20044862

The quality of retiree's lives

Barnes, H, Parry, J, and Lakey, J, *Forging a New Future: The Experiences and Expectations of People Leaving Paid Work over 50* (Policy Press for the Joseph Rowntree Foundation, 2002)

Hodkinson, P, Ford, G, Hodkinson, H, and Hawthorn, R, 'Retirement as a Learning Process' in *Educational Gerontology* (2008; 34; pp 167–184)

Nazroo, J, 'Ethnic Inequalities in Quality of Life at Older Ages' (Economic and Social Research Council, 2005); www.esrc.ac.uk/my-esrc/grants/L480254020/read

Vickerstaff, S, Baldock, J, Cox, J, and Keen, L, *Happy Retirement? The Impact of Employer Policies and Practice on the Process of Retirement* (Policy Press for the Joseph Rowntree Foundation, 2004)

Chapter 2: On Not Falling off a Cliff: Decisions about Leaving Employment
Retirement choices and pensions

Barings, 'No Retirement for One in Ten UK Adults' (2010); www.barings.com/ucm/groups/public/documents/marketingmaterials/063456.pdf

Barnes, H, Parry, J, and Lakey, J, *Forging a New Future: The Experiences and Expectations of People Leaving Paid Work over 50* (Policy Press for the Joseph Rowntree Foundation, 2002)

Carers UK, 'Facts about Carers' (2012); www.carersuk.org/professionals/resources/briefings/item/2729-facts-about-carers-2012

Daily Mail, 'Recession Leaves Fewer Confident of Retirement Plans (*Mail* online, 17 August 2010); www.dailymail.co.uk/money/article-1303846/Recession-leaves-fewer-confident-retirement-plans.html

Department for Work & Pensions, 'Older Workers Statistical Information Booklet' (published annually); www.dwp.gov.uk

Hirsch, D, *Crossroads after 50: Improving Choices in Work and Retirement* (Joseph Rowntree Foundation, 2003)

National Association of Pension Funds, 'Over-50s Set to Live Longer but Not Prosper' (2012)

National Statistics Online, 'Labour Market: Unemployment and Older People in the Labour Market' (25 March 2011)

NHS, 'Survey of Carers in Households 2009/10' (Health and Social Care Information Centre, 2010); www.hscic.gov.uk/pubs/carersurvey0910

Trades Union Congress and Chartered Institute of Personnel and Development, 'Managing Age' (new edition) (Chartered Institute of Personnel and Development, 2011)

Yeomans, L, 'An Update on the Literature on Age and Employment' (HSE, 2011)

Caring in retirement

BBC News Business, 'Default Retirement Age of 65 to End, Ministers Confirm' (13 January 2011); www.bbc.co.uk/news/business-12177927

BBC News, '"I Was in Tears": Carers Tell Their Stories' (11 May 2013); www.bbc.co.uk/news/health-22493627

Griggs, J, *Protect, Support, Provide: Examining the Role of Grandparents in Families at Risk of Poverty* (Grandparents Plus and the Equality and Human Rights Commission, 2010)

Khan, K, 'Employment of the Older Generation' in *Economic and Labour Market Review* (2009; 3: (4); pp 30–36)

Remnick, D, 'Philip Roth Says Enough' (*The New Yorker*, 9 November 2012); www.newyorker.com/online/blogs/books/2012/11/philip-roth-retires-from-novels.html

Chapter 3: Not by Workers Alone: Employers and Workers' Retirement

Chartered Institute of Personnel and Development, 'Employers Are "Missing a Trick" if They Fail to Offer Flexibility to Older Workers' (4 December 2012)

Department for Work & Pensions, 'Older Workers Statistical Information Booklet' (2011)

Harper, S, Khan, HTA, Saxena, A, and Leeson, G, 'Attitudes and Practices of Employers towards Ageing Workers: Evidence from a Global Survey on the Future of Retirement' in *Ageing Horizons* (2006; 5; pp 31–41)

Harper, S, and Marcus, S, 'Age-Related Capacity Decline: A Review of some Workplace Implications' in *Ageing Horizons* (2006; 5; pp 20–30)

International Longevity Centre-UK, 'Gradual Retirement and Pensions Policy' (November 2011)

Macleod, A, Worman, D, Wilton, P, Woodman, P, and Hitchings, P, *Managing an Ageing Workforce: How Employers Are Adapting to an Older Labour Market* (Chartered Management Institute and Chartered Institute of Personnel and Development, September 2010)

Maitland, S, *Working Better: The Over-50s, the New Work Generation* (Equality and Human Rights Commission, 2010); www.equalityhumanrights.com/workingbetter)

National Association of Pension Funds, 'Over-50s Set to Live Longer but Not Prosper' (30 November 2012)

Noone, JH, Stephens, C, and Alpass, FM, 'Preretirement Planning and Well-Being in Later Life' in *Research on Aging* (2009; 31; pp 295–317)

Phillipson, C, and Smith, A, 'Extending Working Life: A Review of the Literature' (Department for Work & Pensions, Research Report 299, 2005)

Stratton, A, 'Training Scheme Sees 900 per cent Rise in Apprenticeships for over-60s' (*Guardian*, 14 November 2011)

Trades Union Congress and Chartered Institute of Personnel and Development, 'Managing Age' (new edition) (Chartered Institute of Personnel and Development, 2011)

Vickerstaff, S, Baldock, J, Cox, J, and Keen, L, *Happy Retirement? The Impact of Employers' Policies and Practices on the Process of Retirement* (Policy Press for the Joseph Rowntree Foundation, 2004)

Watson, R, Manthorpe, E, and Andrews, J, *Nurses Over 50: Options,*

Decisions and Outcomes (Policy Press for the Joseph Rowntree Foundation, 2003)

Yeomans, L, 'An Update on the Literature on Age and Employment' (HSE, 2011)

Chapter 4: Learning *through* Retirement

Biesta, GJJ, Field, J, Hodkinson, J, Macleod, F, and Goodson, IF, *Improving Learning through the Lifecourse* (Routledge, 2011)

Bridges, W, *Transitions: Making Sense of Life's Changes* (Perseus Books, 1980)

Frank, A, *The Wounded Storyteller: Body, Illness and Ethics* (University of Chicago Press, 1995)

Freire, P, *Pedagogy of the Oppressed* (Penguin, 1972)

Giddens, A, *Modernity and Self-Identity* (Polity Press, 1991)

Goodson, IF, and Gill, SR, *Narrative Pedagogy: Life History and Learning* (Peter Lang, 2011)

Hodkinson, H, 'Learning to Work no Longer: Exploring "Retirement"' in *Journal of Workplace Learning* (2010; 22; pp 94–103)

Hodkinson, P, Ford, G, Hodkinson, H, and Hawthorn R, 'Retirement as a Learning Process' in *Educational Gerontology* (2008; 34; pp 167–184)

International Commission on Education for the Twenty-First Century, 'Learning: The Treasure Within' (1996)

Marton, F, Dall'Alba, G, and Beaty, E 'Conceptions of Learning' in *International Journal of Educational Research* (1993; 19:(3); pp 277–300)

Mezirow, J, 'A Critical Theory of Adult Learning and Education' in *Adult Education Quarterly* (1981; 32: (1); pp 3–24)

Reitzes, D, and Mutran, E, 'Lingering Identities in Retirement' in *The Sociology Quarterly* (2006; 47; pp 333–359)

Rogers, C, 'The Formative Tendency' in *Journal of Humanistic Psychology* (1978; 18: (23); p 26)

Vaill, P, *Learning as a Way of Being: Strategies for Survival in a World of Permanent White Water* (Jossey-Bass, 1996)

Chapter 5: Occupation 'Retired'

Age UK, 'Older People as Volunteers: Evidence Review' (2012)

The Archbishop of Canterbury, 'Debate on Older People: Their Place and Contribution in Society' (14 December 2012)

Hirsch, D, *Crossroads After 50: Improving Choices in Work and Retirement* (Joseph Rowntree Foundation, 2003)

Humphrey, A, Lee, L, and Green, R, 'Aspirations for Later Life' (Department for Work & Pensions, Research Report 737, 2011)

Merrick, J, Chorley, M, and Brown, J, 'Introducing the Wellderly' (*The Independent on Sunday*, 20 May 2012)

Smith, JD, and Gay, P, *Active Ageing in Active Communities: Volunteering and the Transition to Retirement* (Policy Press for the Joseph Rowntree Foundation, 2005)

Volunteering

Bubb, S, 'From Dependence to Participation' (*Guardian* supplement 'Making a Difference', 17 October 2009)

WRVS, 'Gold Age Pensioners: Valuing the Socio-Economic Contribution of Older People in the UK' (2011)

Quality and purpose of life

Beckford, M, 'Making Music Key to Happy Retirement, Research Says' (*Telegraph*, 24 November 2011); www.telegraph.co.uk/health/elderhealth/8910445/Making-music-key-to-happy-retirement-research-says.html

Gladwin, B, 'I Graduated Aged 90 – You're Never too Old to Learn' (*Guardian*, 29 May 2012); www.theguardian.com/commentisfree/2012/may/29/graduated-aged-90-bertie-gladwin

Monahan, J, and Clancy, J, 'Lifelong Learning is the Secret to Happiness in Old Age' (*Guardian,* 17 May 2011); www.theguardian.com/adult-learning/lifelong-learning-key-to-happiness

Schnell, T, 'Existential Indifference: Another Quality of Meaning in Life' in *Journal of Humanistic Psychology* (2010; 50: (3), p 351)

Chapter 6: A Little Help from My Friends?

Anderson, M, Li, Y, Bechhofer, F, McCrone, D, and Stewart, R, 'Sooner Rather than Later? Younger and Middle-Aged Adults Preparing for Retirement' in *Ageing and Society* (2000; 20; pp 445–466)

Bourdieu, P, 'The Forms of Capital' in Richardson, J (ed), *Handbook of Theory and Research for the Sociology of Education* (Greenwood, 1986)

Higgs, P, Mein, G, Ferrie, J, Hydeand, M, and Nazroo, J, 'Pathways to Early Retirement: Structure and Agency in Decision-Making among British Civil Servants' in *Ageing and Society* (2003; 23; pp 761–778)

Hofstede, G, *Culture's Consequences: International Differences in Work-Related Values* (Sage, 1980)

Humphreys, K, and Rappaport, J, 'Researching Self-Help/Mutual Aid Groups and Organizations: Many Roads, One Journey' in *Applied and Preventive Psychology* (1994; 3; pp 217–231)

Jones, IR, Leontowitsch, M, and Higgs, P, 'The Experience of Retirement in Second Modernity' in *Sociology* (2010; 44; pp 103–120)

King, SA, 'The Therapeutic Value of Virtual Self-Help Groups' (2004) (unpublished dissertation presented to the Faculty of Pacific Graduate School of Psychology, Palo Alto, California)

Levinson, D, Rush, JC, Peacock, AC, and Milkovich, GT, *The Seasons of a Man's Life* (Knopf, 1978)

Nazroo, J, 'Ethnic Inequalities in Quality of Life at Older Ages' (Economic and Social Research Council, Research L480254020, 2002); www.esrcsocietytoday.ac.uk

Rheingold, H, *The Virtual Community: Homesteading on the Electronic Frontier* (Addison-Wesley, 1993)

Scott, S, 'The Grieving Soul in the Transformation Process' in *New Directions for Adult and Continuing Education* (Jossey-Bass Publishers, 1997)

Sparks, S, 'Exploring Electronic Social Support Groups' in *American Journal of Nursing* (December 1992; pp 62–65)

Chapter 7: *Could-you-just?* Communicating with Family and Friends

Barnes, H, and Parry, J, 'Renegotiating Identity and Relationships: Men and Women's Adjustments to Retirement' in *Ageing and Society* (2004; 24; pp 213–233)

Baxter, LA, 'A Dialectical Perspective of Communication Strategies in Relationship Development' in Duck, S (ed) *Handbook of Personal Relationships*, pp 257–273 (Wiley, 1988)

Kay, F, *The Good Non-Retirement Guide* (Kogan Page, 2011)

Rawlins, WK, 'A Dialectical Analysis of the Tensions, Functions and Strategic Challenges of Communication in Young Adult Friendships' in Anderson, JA (ed) *Communication Yearbook 12*, pp 157–189 (Sage, 1988)

Chapter 8: Three Communities and More: Enriching Your Social Networks

Baumeister, RF, and Leary, MR, 'The Need to Belong: Desire for Interpersonal Attachments as a Fundamental Human Motivation' in *Psychological Bulletin* (1995; 117: (3); pp 497–529)

Crease, Robert P, 'A Retirement Community for University Staff' (*Physics World*, 5 July 2006); http://physicsworld.com/cws/article/print/2006/jul/05/critical-point-the-retirement-problem

Fiske, ST, *Social Beings: A Core Motives Approach to Social Psychology* (Wiley, 2004)

Lodge, C, and Carnell, E, 'Retired, but Still a Physicist' in *Physics World* (February 2011); www.iop.org/careers/workinglife/articles/page-48270.html

Maslow, A, *Motivation and Personality* (Harper and Row, 1970)

McMillan, DW, and Chavis, DM, 'Sense of Community: A Definition and Theory' in *Journal of Community Psychology* (1986; 14: (1); pp 6–23)

Rheingold, H, *The Virtual Community* (1993); www.rheingold.com/vc/book/

University of Gothenburg, 'More People Active Online Now than in the Past' (*Science Daily*, 12 June 2009); www.sciencedaily.com/releases/2009/06/090610074159.htm

Chapter 9: Is Retirement Good for Your Health?

Bamia, C, Trichopoulou, A, and Trichopoulos, D, 'Age at Retirement and Mortality in a General Population Sample – The Greek EPIC Study' in *American Journal of Epidemiology* (2008; 167: (5); pp 561–569)

Benito-Leon J, Bermejo-Pareja, F, and Vega, SL (eds), 'Total Daily Sleep Duration and the Risk of Dementia: A Prospective Population-Based Study' in *European Journal of Neurology* (2009, 16: (9); pp 990–997)

Borgonovi, F, 'Doing Well by Doing Good: The Relationship between Formal Volunteering and Self-Reported Health and Happiness' in *Social Science and Medicine* (June 2008; 66: (11), pp 2321–2334); http://eprints.lse.ac.uk/24592/

Campbell, D, 'Northerners "20% More Likely to Die Under 75" than Southerners' (*Guardian*, 15 February 2011); www.theguardian.com/society/2011/feb/15/people-in-north-die-younger, quoting a study by Manchester University and Manchester City Council

Fabian Society UK, 'Costs of the Ageing Society' (March 2010); www.fabians.org.uk

Kolata, G, 'A Surprising Secret to Long Life: Stay in School' (*New York Times*, 3 Janary 2007); www.nytimes.com/2007/01/03/health/03aging.html, quoting a study by Dr Adriana Lleras-Muney (Princeton University)

Malta , S, 'Social Connectedness and Health Amongst Older Adults' (TASA Conference, University of Tasmania 6–8 December 2005); www.tasa.org.au/conferences/conferencepapers05/papers per cent20(pdf)/health_malta.pdf

Mein, G, Martikainen, P, Hemingway, H, Stansfeld, S, and Marmot, M, 'Is Retirement Good or Bad for Mental and Physical Health Functioning? Whitehall II Longitudinal Study of Civil Servants' in *British Medical Journal* (2003; 57; pp 46–49)

Sahlgren, GH, 'Work Longer, Live Healthier: The Relationship between Economic Activity, Heath and Government Policy' (Institute of Economic Affairs and Age Endeavour Fellowship, Discussion paper No 46, 2013)

Slevin, KF, and Wingrove, CR, 'Women in Retirement: A Review and Critique of Empirical Research since 1976' in *Sociological Inquiry* (1995; 65: (1); pp 1–21)

Stibich, M, 'Is Retirement Good for You?' (2009); longevity.about. com/od/healthyagingandlongevity/a/retirement.htm

Sunstein, C, and Thaler, R, *Nudge: Improving Decisions about Health, Wealth, and Happiness* (Yale University Press, 2008)

Tsai, SP, Wendt, JK, Donnelly, RP, de Jong, G, and Ahmed, FS, 'Age at Retirement and Long Term Survival of an Industrial Population: Prospective Cohort Study' in *British Medical Journal* (27 October 2005); www.bmj.com/content/331/7523/995.full

Westerlund, H, 'Job Satisfaction and Working Conditions Must Be Improved to Keep Older Workers in the Workforce' (Sweden's National Institute for Psychosocial Factors and Health, 2009); www.eurekalert.org/pub_releases/2009-11/l-jsa110509.php

Chapter 10: The Spaces You Live in

'Hedge Fund Industry Review: Key Market H1 Monitor Report' (July 2011); www.hedgeindex.com

Hill, K, Kellard, K, Middleton, S, Cox, L, and Pound, E, *Understanding Resources in Later Life*, chapter 2, p 9 (Joseph Rowntree Foundation, 2007)

Kay, F, *The Good Non-Retirement Guide* (Kogan Page, 2011)

Miller, J, *Crazy Age: Thoughts on Being Old* (Virago, 2010)

Chapter 11: This *Is* Your Rainy Day: Relationships with Money

Steiner, S, 'Over 45? You're about to Get Happier …' (*Guardian*, 13 March 2012); www.theguardian.com/lifeandstyle/2012/mar/13/new-happiness-study-older-people

Chapter 12: Wonder and Awe: The Time of Your Life

Best, R, 'Emotion, Spiritual Experience and Education: A Reflection' in *International Journal of Children's Spirituality* (2011; 16: (4), pp 361–368)

Copsey, K, *From the Ground Up: Understanding the Spiritual World of the Child* (Barnabas, 2005)

Dunford, M, *Make the Most of your Time on Earth: A Rough Guide to the World* (Penguin, 2010)

Heller, J, *Catch-22* (Jonathan Cape, 1955)

Kumar, S, *No Destination* (Green Books, 2004). Satish Kumar was interviewed by Vidal, J, 'Soul Man' (*Guardian*, 16 January 2008); www.theguardian.com/environment/2008/jan/16/activists

Rogers, CR, *A Way of Being* (Houghton Mifflin Co, 1980)

Steiner, S, 'Top Five Regrets of the Dying' (*Guardian*, 1 February 2012); www.theguardian.com/lifeandstyle/2012/feb/01/top-five-regrets-of-the-dying

Index